An Object-Oriented Library for Shared-Memory Parallel Simulations

Philip Machanick

Thesis Presented for the Degree of

DOCTOR OF PHILOSOPHY

in the Department of Computer Science

UNIVERSITY OF CAPE TOWN

April 1996

final revisions: October 1996

minor updates: June 2008, December 2012

National Library of Australia Cataloguing-in-Publication entry

Author: Machanick, Philip, 1957-

Title: An object-oriented library for shared-memory parallel

            simulations / Philip Machanick.

Edition: 2nd ed.

ISBN: 978-0-9804510-2-3 (pbk.)

Notes: Bibliography.

Subjects: Microprocessors.
            Object-oriented programming (Computer science)
            Memory management (Computer science)

Dewey Number: 004.35

Other RAMpage Research books by this author:

No Tomorrow – novel: climate change theme
ISBN-10: 0980451019   ISBN-13: 978-0-9804510-1-6

Abstract

Programming shared-memory multiprocessor systems is becoming increasingly difficult as the gap between memory speed and processor speed increases. At the same time, this class of computer—based on standard microprocessors—is becoming increasingly common as an alternative to traditional mainframes and supercomputers.

Programs that are not sympathetic to caches can perform poorly on such systems. Problems include *false sharing* (unrelated data in a cache block, resulting in coherence misses), inadequate *blocking* (processing data as often as possible before it moves out of the cache) and poor exploitation of *prefetch* (fetching data before it is needed).

This research addresses the problem of accommodating changes in memory hierarchy cost and cache characteristics through an object-oriented C++ library called OOSH (Object-Oriented Library for Shared Memory). OOSH includes low-level allocators which pad and align objects to cache block boundaries, and primitives for launching processes, locking and synchronization. OOSH also provides support for *object blocking*—an object-oriented version of blocking, a technique traditionally used in matrix operations. Blocking divides an algorithm's data into blocks or *tiles*, which are processed as far as possible before moving on to other data, with the objective of reducing cache misses.

Performance of OOSH is evaluated by running selected applications from the Stanford SPLASH benchmarks on the Mint MIPS architecture simulator. Simulations are run both with parameters similar to current multiprocessor architectures, and with higher memory hierarchy costs, to investigate the impact of technology trends. OOSH versions of the applications are compared with the SPLASH implementations, based on Argonne National Laboratories Parmacs macros.

The applications are MP3D (particle-based wind tunnel simulation), Barnes-Hut (*n*-body gravitation simulation) and Water (water molecule simulation). MP3D only needs local synchronization, and uses *distributed synchronization*: barriers are replaced by synchronization on local clocks in regions of space. Early versions of MP3D are poorly written in terms of their cache behaviour, and the OOSH version of MP3D is substantially rewritten. To provide another data point with fewer variables, Barnes-Hut is a useful application. Although it has relatively complex data structures and algorithms, and is well-suited to object-oriented implementation, so the OOSH version is relatively similar to the SPLASH version. Water is a straightforward program which is used to investigate the performance impact of OOSH if no attempt is made to improve the structure of the application or its data, i.e., there are even fewer variables than in the case of the re-implementation of Barnes-Hut.

OOSH is shown to give improved cache usage for programs that are rewritten to exploit its features, especially in the case of MP3D which is substantially rewritten. The improvement in cache behaviour is shown to be significant, even for Barnes-Hut which has substantially the same structure for both SPLASH and OOSH versions. Water, which is not significantly rewritten, is shown to suffer a performance drop of up to 9% as a result of the overhead of object-oriented constructs. By comparison, the OOSH version of Barnes-Hut, on a simulated 32-processor architecture with a cache miss cost of 100 clock cycles, is about 20% faster than the SPLASH version.

Object blocking is shown to be a relatively minor effect in MP3D. Object blocking could be a useful optimization for simulations with a larger number of references to one object per timestep than is the case for MP3D. However, this research shows cache block aligned memory access to be a big win, and is more likely to be a useful optimization than blocking, across a variety of applications.

In general, as memory hierarchy costs increase, OOSH is shown to become increasingly beneficial, and even an application like Barnes-Hut, which had a relatively low number of misses before being ported to OOSH, can gain significantly from cache block aligned memory allocators.

Acknowledgments

I would like to thank my supervisor Henk Goosen for providing financial support out of his FRD grant. I would also like to thank David Cheriton for supporting me on three visits to the Distributed Systems Group, Computer Science Department, Stanford University, during which the ground work for this PhD research was laid.

My first Stanford trip was sponsored in part by the Mellon Foundation and the Anderson-Capelli Fund, and I also received support at Stanford while working with David Cheriton from DARPA contract N00014–88–K–0619.

The University of the Witwatersrand granted me a total of 15 months' unpaid leave, in addition to two sabbaticals totaling 15 months. Without this time this work would not have been possible.

I would like to thank Ronnie Apteker of The Internet Solution for giving me access to a commercial system with faster international internet access, without which timing runs for the later stages of the research would have been more difficult.

Hugh Holbrook assisted with work on the MP3D application at Stanford, and did measurements of the difference between distributed synchronization and barriers, as well as TLB effects in an implementation of MP3D. Jeff McDonald of Silicon Graphics (then at NASA-Ames) supplied the original version of MP3D and was very helpful in explaining the physics of the simulation. James Winget of Silicon Graphics ran and timed several versions of MP3D on a Silicon Graphics multiprocessor machine. Stephen Goldschmidt and Helen Davis gave advice on the use of their Tango simulator used during earlier work conducted at Stanford.

Dieter Polzin implemented most of the Chiron performance visualizer that was used in this research. Peter Hinz put in a large amount of effort in helping to use Chiron, and added new features that were useful in isolating performance problems.

My external examiners, Josep Torrellas, John Mashey and Kai Li, provided useful comments that helped to improve the final thesis.

Finally, I must thank Ian Sanders for his useful comments on an early draft of the thesis.

Preface to Updated Edition

Since I completed this thesis in 1996 a few things have changed. C++ has become a mainstream language, and shared-memory multiprocessors have become commodity devices, rather than high-end computation devices, in the form of multicore processors.

A few things though have not changed. The CPU-memory speed gap is still widening. Multicore designs reduce some of the effect by sharing lower-level caches or at least (if designed for performance) reducing overheads of invalidations by doing cache-to-cache transfers, rather than having to go through DRAM. At worst, they have some savings on transactions through an external bus.

In some respects, therefore, this thesis is as relevant today as when I did the original work more than ten years ago.

Why would anyone read this thesis today? Because much of this was new at the time, I explained some things in greater detail (e.g., features of C++) than you would in a thesis today. Although this is not beginner material, anyone with a little background in programming and computer architecture should be able to understand it.

What would you do differently today? You would probably steer clear of system-specific primitives like SGI's `sproc` system call. You may also feel tempted to use features of C++ that were either non-existent or not fully formed at the time I did this work, like templates or the STL library. Nonetheless, I hope some will find my approach using a more primitive version of the language easier to follow than one using templates.

What else might jar the modern reader? At the time I did my coding, the conventions for C++ source file naming hadn't settled out, and I ended my source files with ".C" where today you would use ".cpp" or ".c++".

Despite these anachronisms, many of the issues explored here are still current, and I hope this work will still be of some use.

Who will benefit from reading this thesis? Anyone wanting insights into the interaction between performance and memory hierarchy should find it interesting. It is not however an academic text or manual. You need to read it with sufficient background, or in conjunction with texts on architecture and possibly algorithms.

Commentary

I've added brief commentaries to most chapters, to relate the material to subsequent developments.

The commentaries generally do not go into much detail. While languages and hardware have moved on, many of the same principles still apply. Understand how your code interacts with the memory system, and you will have a significant advantage over a mere hacker – even one well schooled in data structures and algorithms lore.

This thesis was written using Microsoft Word 5.0, much to my regret, as reformatting it in book size with a later version of Word has been a fraught experience. You may notice for example that commentary boxes that appear at the head of a page have no top border, a problem I gave up trying to remedy. The odd picture or footnote instead of going above the page footer overlapped it – for no obvious reason (why did the others not have this problem?). Every PhD I do in future will be written up using LaTeX.

— Philip Machanick, Brisbane, 2008

Contents

1. Introduction

1.1 The Problem

It is becoming crucial for high-performance applications to address the growing processor-memory speed gap [Hennessy and Jouppi 1991]. Consequently, it is becoming increasingly essential to make efficient usage of caches, which are used in most computer systems today to bridge the processor-memory speed gap. While some supercomputers do not use caches, cache-based shared memory systems are capturing an increasing share of the market [Lewis 1994]. The research reported on in this thesis investigates optimizations which reduce memory traffic in shared-memory systems, by being sensitive to caches. Time-stepped simulations—an important category of performance-critical application—are used in measurements of the effectiveness of the strategy adopted (though the approach applies to other applications).

Another motivation for the research is the mismatch between the processor-memory speed gap, and the additional growing trend towards object-oriented programming. The mismatch arises because most work on automatic or compiler optimizations that reduce memory access costs assume FORTRAN-like semantics [Bacon *at al*. 1994].

One study has shown that attempting to write C++ in a FORTRAN-like style, using arrays implemented as vector classes, can result in poor performance [Haney

1994]. However, there are problem areas where object-oriented implementation is natural, and traditional FORTRAN features are not applicable—typically, relatively irregular data structures, or problems in which the layout of data in memory evolves as the program executes. It seems pointless to attempt to beat a mature technology like FORTRAN at areas where it is strongest; instead this thesis emphasizes development of techniques for areas suited to object-oriented methods.

Processing part of a data set that is small enough to fit into a cache as far as possible before moving on is called *blocking* or *tiling*—and is commonly applied to array or matrix algorithms [Lam *et al.* 1991; Demmel and Higham 1992]. The idea of blocking is extended in the work reported on here to object-oriented code, which is called *object blocking* in this thesis. Object blocking is implemented in space-based applications by dividing space into *precincts*. Each precinct is processed as fully as possible, before moving to the next.

While object blocking may not apply to all applications—and in fact did not produce convincing results in those measured here—a more obvious optimization is to ensure that all data structures are padded and aligned to cache blocks. At the cost of some wasted memory, padded aligned allocation avoids an important problem, *false sharing*. False sharing is the situation where two processors access the same cache block, and at least one of them writes to the block, but neither processor in fact uses the same data.

More detailed discussion of optimizations is deferred to section 1.3, where cache concepts—needed to understand the optimizations—are explained.

In general, applications with properties common to particle-based simulations—i.e., spatial locality, but with state that migrates in time—have the potential to gain from object blocking and other optimizations introduced in this thesis. The research reported on here therefore examine the possibility of developing an efficient strategy for particle-based simulations, and any other applications with similar characteristics.

Other solutions to the problem of writing efficient parallel applications which do work for object-oriented code include special-purpose languages such as COOL [Chandra *et al.* 1994] and class libraries [Bershad *et al.* 1988; Beck 1990]. Special-purpose languages have two major drawbacks: it is relatively difficult to add new features, and they are not as portable as class libraries. If care is taken in writing a class library, machine-dependent aspects may be isolated to a small module. Other work on class libraries however has not addressed the processor-memory speed gap, which has been identified as a major issue for this research.

The focus of the thesis therefore is investigation of cache-sensitive optimizations that may be effected relatively easily using a object-oriented library. In this way, using an object-oriented language can be turned to advantage—by contrast with the position where an object-oriented language inhibits existing optimization strategies.

It is not surprising to find that object-oriented code is common in simulations, since the first object-oriented language, Simula-67 [Dahl *et al.* 1970], was designed for implementing simulations. Much work on implementing parallel and distributed simulations [Fujimoto 1990], for example, is done in C++.

Most work on general scientific computation is still done in FORTRAN*, but there is some movement towards C++ for some scientific computations, such as grid generation [Dener 1992]. In another example, in the 1990 Conference on Computing in High Energy Physics, there were only two papers on object-oriented programming; by the 1994 conference on the same topic, there were eleven.

If it can be shown that a class library can be used to efficiently program a shared-memory multiprocessor system, the existing hesitant tendency towards expanding the realm of object-oriented code from simulations to a broader range of scientific applications would be encouraged.

1.2 Structure of Chapter

The following section (1.3) contains a more detailed discussion of caches—which is intended to make the rationale for the research clearer. In addition, hardware strategies for hiding latency are briefly covered in this next section, for additional background.

Once background has been established, this introductory chapter goes on to explain the approach adopted to the research in more detail, in section 1.4.

Section 1.5 describes the contribution of the research in detail.

The chapter concludes with a road map of the rest of the thesis, in section 1.6.

---

* For example, almost all algorithms published in *ACM Transactions on Mathematical Software* (if a specific language is used) are written in FORTRAN.

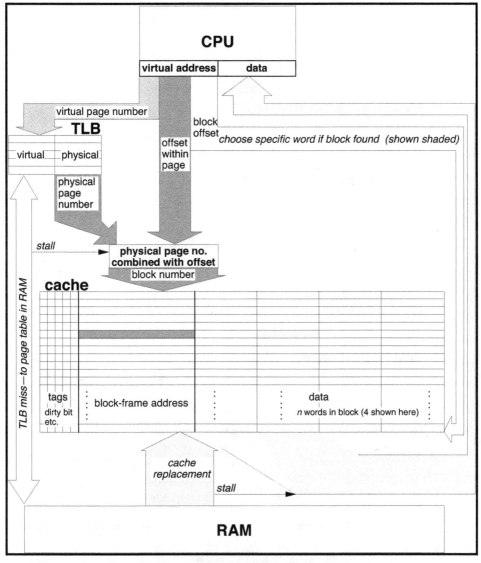

Figure 1.1 A Cache with a TLB

data and control flow for a memory read is shown

1.3 Caches

This section presents a general overview of caches. First, a brief overview of general

principles is presented, followed by a summary of major causes of misses. Then,

techniques for reducing misses are summarized.

In addition to the cache itself, an important element of the hierarchy is the *translation lookaside buffer* (TLB), a small specialized cache of recent page address translations. Although the impact of the TLB is not considered until future work is covered in 8.2, it is useful to understand how virtual memory relates to caches, so a summary of address translation issues is presented.

Although not of direct relevance to this research, for completeness, write strategies, as related to shared-memory multiprocessor systems, are described. In conclusion, issues specific to multiprocessor systems, of more relevance to this thesis, are outlined.

Figure 1.1 is a stylized view of a uniprocessor cache-based memory hierarchy.

1.3.1 Cache Organization

Detail in actual architectures may differ, but the general principles are common to most current architectures; for a general overview, see Smith [1982].

The purpose of the cache is primarily to avoid references to a much bigger slower memory—which may be the main memory, or another level of cache.

A cache is not only a faster form of memory, but is also organized in a different way to ordinary RAM; the organization of the cache therefore has to be considered when attempting to understand cache behaviour. Cache organization is important for uniprocessor systems, but multiprocessor systems can introduce extra complications [Tullsen and Eggers 1993].

A cache is organized into blocks (also called lines). A block is usually the smallest unit that can be fetched from or written back to slower memory. Another usual property of caches is that a block can either only go in one location (a direct-mapped cache) or a small number of locations (set-associative cache).

Since a cache is smaller than the slower memory the level below, it generally contains a subset of the information in the slower memory. An attempt at referencing in the cache may therefore result in a *miss*.

1.3.2 Causes of Misses

There are several possible reasons for a miss [Hennessy and Patterson 1995]:

- *compulsory* (or *cold start*)—the block hasn't been referenced before and is therefore not in the cache

- *capacity*—the block has been referenced before but has been *replaced* by another block because the cache isn't big enough to hold all the blocks referenced since the given block was previously referenced

- *conflict* (or *interference*)—since blocks usually can only go in one or a limited number of locations (depending on the cache's associativity), two or more blocks may map to the same location in the cache and force each other out— even if a capacity miss would not have occurred

- *coherence*—the block is no longer consistent with another level of memory, and becomes *invalid*. In a multiprocessor system, a coherence miss occurs if another processor writes to the block. Even in uniprocessors, there can be coherence misses if input devices can write into a program's address space

1.3.3 Reduction of Misses

Compulsory misses may be reduced if cache blocks are made larger. On the other hand, capacity misses may increase if blocks are made larger, as a higher number of blocks is likely to contain parts which are not referenced. Choosing a block size is partially a matter of balancing *spatial locality* (memory near a specific reference is likely to be referenced soon) with *temporal locality* (a specific location is likely to be referenced again some time soon after a specific reference).

Large blocks favour spatial locality; small blocks favour temporal locality. However, as cache sizes increase, large blocks become less of a liability, especially on uniprocessor systems where coherence misses are not a serious problem [Hennessy and Patterson 1995]. Memory generally has the property that starting an access takes a lot longer than the actual transfer. Also, memory can be organized into multiple banks so that each bank is ready to start delivering or receiving as the previous bank completes its transfer; this too makes moving larger blocks more efficient.

Larger blocks are also a way of achieving *prefetch*: fetching data or instructions before they are needed. However, there's a limit to how big a cache block can be expected to have a useful prefetch effect (the optimum size depends on the application). Another way of achieving prefetch is to have explicit prefetch instructions. A prefetch instruction does not stall when the data it references is not found in the cache, since it does not actually use the data. The Stanford DASH multiprocessor system, for example, has non-binding prefetch instructions: if the prefetched data is written to by another processor before it's used, it is invalidated and has to be fetched again [Lenoski *et al*. 1992].

Another strategy for prefetch is to use a prefetch buffer. Blocks which have been prefetched are not immediately brought into the cache, but are stored in a separate small cache. This way, if the prefetch is inaccurate, prefetched blocks do not displace other needed blocks [Jouppi 1990].

Placement of data can have a marked impact on the number of conflict misses. Consequently, reducing conflict misses has been the subject of a number of studies— not only on shared-memory systems [Bershad *et al*. 1992; Bacon *et al*. 1994]. Since a relatively simple hardware technique can reduce conflict misses—and conflict misses are less of an issue with large caches, this thesis does not consider software strategies for reducing conflict misses in detail. The hardware strategy is the use of a small fully associative cache containing blocks recently replaced, so that they can be moved back to the cache quickly. This *miss cache* strategy has been shown to be effective in removing the costs of conflict misses even in small direct-mapped caches [Jouppi 1990].

Blocking is the strategy of reducing capacity misses by attempting to do as much work as possible on data which fits into a cache before moving on to other data [Lam *at al*. 1991]. In the work described in this thesis, blocking is combined with processor affinity: not only is a given part of a simulation's data set processed as much as possible before moving on to another part of the data set, but the work is done as far as possible on the same processor.

Another area where coherence misses can be a problem is with implementation of synchronization primitives, such as locks [Weber and Gupta 1989]. There has already been considerable work on efficient strategies for synchronization primitives [Mellor-Crumney and Scott 1991; Lenoski *et al.* 1992; Galles and Williams 1994], so this thesis does not place heavy emphasis on synchronization primitives designed to reduce cache misses.

1.3.4 Address Translation and Caches

Whenever a CPU issues an address (whether for a data or an instruction reference), the address must be translated from a virtual address to a physical address. This translation is done using page tables which are stored in ordinary memory. However, if a cache is intended to replace references to ordinary memory as often as possible by references to a faster cache memory, page translations cannot be done from a table in ordinary memory. In fact, page translations need to be faster than cache references, otherwise a cache reference would be held up waiting for the page translation. Hence the need for a TLB—a small fast cache of recent page translations.

Most current architectures have a relatively small TLB. A smaller TLB (or any cache for that matter) is easier to make fast, and it is possible to use a relatively small TLB on the principle that page translations, once done, will be used often. Recent designs have a few hundred entries in the TLB; designs of the early 1990s typically had 30 to 100 [Nagle *et al.* 1993].

Pages are typically 4K or 8K on a wide variety of systems, and if memory references are largely sequential, the assumption that a small TLB is acceptable is correct. The assumption is most likely to be true of code processing arrays in relatively sequential fashion, or of code with tight loops with relatively few data references.

Some architectures, such as the MIPS R4000 and its successors [Kane and Heinrich 1992], look up the tag in the cache using the virtual address. The physical address is still stored still with the tag. This organization means that it is possible for the TLB to deliver its translation slightly later in the cache reference cycle.

Some have advocated purely virtually addressed caches [Cheriton *at al*. 1986], to avoid the complications the TLB introduces.

However, a virtually addressed cache introduces other problems, such as complications of dealing with aliases (more than one virtual address which refers to the same physical page, as in the copy on write feature of some operating systems such as Mach). Although solutions to these problems have been proposed [Cheriton *at al*. 1986; Goodman 1987; Wheeler and Bershad 1992; Inouye *et al*. 1992], virtually addressed caches are not in wide use (exceptions include some SPARC and HP PA systems).

Consequently, any undesirable interactions with the TLB should be considered in any future strategy for reducing memory hierarchy costs. Since the research presented here is focused on cache issues, potential TLB problems are only taken up again when future research is discussed in the final chapter.

Another aspect of the memory hierarchy which is peripheral to the research reported here, but is mentioned in the further work section in the concluding chapter, is management of a page cache. A page cache is a cache of pages which have been replaced, but which are still resident in memory. There is a move in operating systems towards allowing user programs to manage the page cache [Harty and Cheriton 1991; Subramanian 1991], which creates some potential for software strategies to further manage memory usage at another level of the memory hierarchy.

1.3.5 Write Policies in Shared-Memory Multiprocessor Systems

There are various strategies for writing cache blocks back to memory. A write through cache was popular with older multiprocessor systems. Immediately as a block became *dirty* (written to and hence different from the corresponding block in the next level of the memory), it was written to the next level down. A write-through strategy is easy to implement, as it is easy to broadcast the updated block to other caches to ensure that they remain consistent. However it is expensive in terms of memory and bus traffic. Consequently, more recent architectures in which the processor speed is greater have tended to move towards a write back strategy, in which a dirty block is only written once it is replaced from the cache [Lovett and Thakkar 1988].

The underlying assumption of a write back strategy—and other alternative write strategies which have been proposed [Joupi 1993]—is that a block will stay in the cache for some time after it has been written, otherwise there is no gain over the write through strategy. However, false sharing or the absence of processor affinity—

both defined in the next subsection—may negate the advantages of a write back strategy.

1.3.6 Other Multiprocessor Issues

Coherence misses are the major focus of this research, since they are often the biggest single cause of memory traffic in parallel programs [Eggers and Katz 1989]. Two major strategies are used in this research: removing *false sharing* and improving *processor affinity*. False sharing occurs when unrelated data referenced by two or more processor is found in the same cache block, and at least one processor writes to the block, forcing unnecessary invalidations. False sharing can be addressed in various ways—some of which are described in Chapter 3—including cache block aligned memory allocation, with padding to ensure that unrelated data is not in the same cache block.

Fetching large blocks—aside from being an potentially inaccurate prefetch strategy—has another negative consequence in multiprocessor systems. If part of a block is not needed by a specific processor, but is written to by another, spurious invalidations result. This is called *false sharing*.

Unfortunately, there are good reasons to use larger blocks on uniprocessor systems even if there are potentially better ways of achieving prefetch—as was noted above where block size was discussed. Given that the growing processor-memory speed gap is rapidly driving up cache sizes (1Mbyte of second-level cache is almost commonplace in 1995), larger blocks are likely to become more common. As early as 1990, the IBM RS/6000 had 128-byte blocks [Bakoglu *et al.* 1990], though 32 bytes was more common for that era.

As long as the same processors are to be used for both uniprocessor and multiprocessor systems, strategies for coping with large blocks, without an unacceptably high number of coherence misses, are required. This research assumes that multiprocessor systems will draw as much as possible on uniprocessor technology for reasons of cost, so reducing false sharing is an important goal.

Small-scale multiprocessor systems typically use *snooping*, in which any change in a cache state that needs to be communicated to other processes is broadcast on the bus, and each processor snoops on the bus to ensure that it keeps its cache consistent. Snooping does not scale up, and directory-based schemes have been widely investigated and implemented as an alternative—for example in the DASH [Lenoski *et al.* 1990], Alewife [Chaiken *et al.* 1991] and ParaDiGM projects [Cheriton *et al.* 1991a]. For this research, it is sufficient to note that scaling shared-memory systems up presents problems in the presence of a high number of misses, whether for snooping or for any directory-based scheme.

1.4 Approach

The major goal of this research is to show that it is possible to address the processor-memory speed gap by using an object-oriented library to provide a starting point for efficient program structure (as well as efficient reusable low-level constructs, such as memory allocators). In particular, the research aims to show that an object-oriented library can provide a basis for implementing optimizations that are similar to those implemented by good optimizing compilers, without resorting to FORTRAN-like idioms (such as putting all data in arrays).

The object-oriented library is designed for applications that can be decomposed into spatial units with mostly local interactions, since such a structure creates opportunities for amortizing the cost of bringing data into a cache. Such application characteristics are reasonably common, especially in code originally designed for distributed memory systems [Hwang *et al.* 1995]. In addition, programs that naturally fit the library's structure may be difficult to program efficiently in a language like FORTRAN, which lacks dynamic data structures and pointers.

In addition to addressing the processor-memory speed gap, this research uses the abstraction capabilities of C++ to demonstrate how machine dependent code may be hidden in a relatively small module. C++ abstraction mechanisms are also used to implement parallel programming constructs, with the aim of reducing the potential for programmer error.

Another aspect of the performance-improvement goal of the research is to show that any higher overhead of C++ method invocation can be offset against more efficient implementation of reusable code, particularly carefully optimized memory allocators. This is in contrast to the largely ad hoc approach of common shared-memory code, for example, as found in the Stanford SPLASH benchmarks [Singh *et al.* 1992b].

A final goal of this research—which applies to the previous goals—is to show that the performance improvements afforded by the strategies implemented in an object-oriented library are likely to become more significant, if the current processor-memory speed gap trend is continued.

The major strategy for realizing these goals is the implementation and evaluation of a C++ library, through performance measurement of a number of time-stepped simulations—with comparison of versions written with and without the library. The library is called OOSH (Object-Oriented Library for Shared Memory). Performance is measured using the Mint MIPS simulator, extended to model a typical modern commercially available shared-memory multiprocessor design such as a high-end Silicon Graphics system. To predict future performance, the simulations are also run with cache miss costs doubled. As a reality check, run times are measured using a real machine, an 8-processor Silicon Graphics 4D/380.

The OOSH approach cannot obtain better performance than an ad hoc approach. However, a cleaner object-oriented implementation should make it easier to do detailed optimization. Also, the low-level shared-memory constructs should be easier to rewrite for new architectures than is the case for ad hoc approaches. Finally, once these constructs have been written for a specific architecture, they can be reused for new applications, or as a basis for porting existing applications that already run on other architectures. The potential benefits therefore are improvement in programmer productivity, less application-specific work on optimization, and improved portability.

Others who have designed shared memory programming constructs have mostly extended languages such as C++ or proposed completely new languages [Wyatt et al. 1992]. This research however accepts the view of others who have found that C++ is sufficiently expressive to provide cleanly structured alternatives to macro processors [Bershad *et al.* 1988; Beck 1990], without the need to invent yet another language with all the problems that introduces for code portability.

The major focus is on containing memory referencing costs by programming sympathetically to the cache architecture. However, to illustrate that generality is not lost by using a library and a standard language, some new synchronization constructs are also investigated.

The SPLASH benchmarks are a reasonable source of applications since they are becoming widely used in the research community and most have been reasonably well optimized. The OOSH library implemented for this research is therefore used to implement a representative sample of the SPLASH benchmarks.

The SPLASH benchmarks used here are MP3D, Barnes-Hut and Water. These programs are chosen to give a reasonably wide range of application characteristics, especially with respect to opportunities for improvement by reimplementing them using OOSH.

MP3D is a particle-based wind tunnel simulation, originally developed for a Cray vector machine [McDonald and Baganoff 1988]. MP3D is chosen for its poor cache behaviour, and its potential for reimplementation using the spatial decomposition strategy supported by the library. The potential for spatial decomposition arises because communication is mostly local.

Barnes-Hut is an *n*-body gravitation simulation [Barnes and Hut 1986]. It uses an octree representation of space to efficiently find bodies that are close enough to a given body to be used individually in the gravitational computation. Bodies that are further away are clustered together and treated as a single body. Barnes-Hut is used as an example of a program which has already been reasonably well optimized. It does not present the same opportunities for improvement as MP3D. The SPLASH code has good cache behaviour, and the algorithm inherently requires more global transfer of information than MP3D, making it less amenable to spatially decomposed restructuring.

Water is a more straightforward program than Barnes-Hut, with a fairly simple structure. Although written in C, it is a simple translation from an earlier FORTRAN version and therefore a useful example of general numeric code. It is a simulation of the dynamics of a system of water molecules. Water is used to measure the overhead of the library on code which does not have an obvious object-oriented implementation, so the library only adds overhead, rather than providing opportunity to use a more efficient structure or primitives. Water can therefore be seen as an illustration of the cost of the library when no significant change is made to the original code.

1.5 Overview of the OOSH Strategy

The OOSH library aims to reduce memory reference costs through two strategies. It provides a framework for writing applications which can be decomposed spatially, to support object blocking and processor affinity, and it provides low-level memory allocators which are sensitive to cache blocks, with the aim of eliminating false sharing.

Spatial decomposition aims to meet two goals: doing all related work together, so cache misses are amortized before data moves out of the cache, and exploiting locality in communication patterns, so that communication between different parts of the application can stay on one processor as far as possible. Inherent in these goals is maintaining *processor affinity*: data should stay with the same processor as far as possible—at least until it would in any case have moved out of the cache. Doing all related work together is an example of *blocking*, which is described more fully in section 3.3. For now, it is worth noting that a difference between *object blocking* in OOSH and in much other work is that OOSH does not require that data be represented in arrays [Lam *et al.* 1991; Bacon *et al.* 1994].

A programmer using OOSH may need to put some work into changing an existing program so that it uses classes which can have their own new operator, which would use the cache-sensitive allocators. A significantly larger amount of work may be needed to restructure the application to exploit spatial decomposition; if there is a high degree of sharing, such effort is worthwhile, in terms of potential performance gain.

OOSH is intended to be portable, and only uses C++ features which are likely to be available in any standard compiler—except for a small machine-dependent module. OOSH provides a few standard primitives, including the ability to launch processes, locks and barriers. Since the aim of the library is to support efficient memory allocation, little work has been put into design of novel or efficient synchronization constructs. One exception is the development of a strategy called *distributed synchronization* [Cheriton *et al.* 1993]. Distributed synchronization is applicable when an application has a decomposition of work which allows nearest neighbours (in space — or any other way in which the application is decomposed) to be used to determine whether a given unit of work may proceed.

The advantage of distributed synchronization is that a processor does not have to spin on a specific lock variable if part of its workload is blocked, waiting for another processor. Instead, the processor which has been blocked moves on to attempt to execute another part of its workload. Even if all of its workload is blocked and the processor effectively spins on the state of nearest neighbours of all of its units of work, the problem of a single lock becoming a hot spot [Weber and Gupta 1989] is avoided.

Where possible, good ideas from previous work have been used. For example, a C++ object has a constructor and a destructor, which are automatically called when the object is respectively created or ceases to exist. OOSH implements a lock using a constructor to set the lock, and a destructor to release it. A programmer therefore does not have to remember to release the lock (which may be an issue, for example, if there is a `break` or `return` statement). This strategy has previously been used in PRESTO, which is described in section 3.4 [Bershad *et al.* 1988].

1.6 Original Contribution

Original contributions of this research are broken down into feasibility demonstration and specific performance measurement.

The feasibility demonstration covers a wider range of features than those which are specifically measured. The reason for implementing a wide range of features is that the specific focus of the research—addressing the processor-memory speed gap—is most credibly addressed by measuring performance of real applications. The performance measurement must also be seen in the context of attempting to support the trend towards object-oriented code, by showing that such code is not an obstacle to good performance. Hence, the OOSH library has to be shown to support features required to implement typical parallel applications (specifically, time-stepped simulations—though many of the techniques could be more generally applied).

Demonstration of feasibility therefore covers the following points:

- optimizations such as object blocking, processor affinity, and padded and aligned allocators can be implemented in a reusable library

- the library can be used for a range of applications with different characteristics

- a range of typical parallel programming constructs can be conveniently implemented, using standard C++ features, especially constructors and destructors (which are useful for setting up and clearing state associated with constructs such as locks and barriers)

- the machine-dependent code can be isolated to a relatively small module to enhance maintainability, portability and adaptability to new architecture concerns

The feasibility aspects are intended to show that the performance measurements are credible, i.e., have some generality. They are not considered to be central to the research, and are therefore not quantified.

Performance measurements are on a simulated system with up to 32-processors, and with the miss cost varied to represent two generations in which the processor-memory speed gap has doubled. In summary, on the 32-processor system, these measurements show that:

- the reusable object-oriented library, OOSH, results in competitive performance—even a reasonably well optimized application, such as the SPLASH version of Barnes-Hut, is shown to gain in speed by up to 20% when reimplemented using OOSH

- biggest gains are to be had from totally reimplementing a poorly structured application, such as MP3D—which gains from spatial decomposition as well as from better memory allocation—where the OOSH version is almost twice as fast as the SPLASH version

- even a fairly small absolute difference in the fraction of invalidations (0.077% on SPLASH Barnes-Hut, versus 0.036% on OOSH Barnes-Hut—which mostly gains from better memory allocation) can make a big difference with high cache miss costs which are becoming increasingly common

- a FORTRAN-like program—such as Water—cannot be expected to gain from a simplistic reimplementation in OOSH. If it cannot be restructured to allocate data and work in a more object-oriented style, performance is more likely to be lost than gained

Also of significance is the difference between the impact of doubling the cache miss cost (from 50 to 100 cycles), on SPLASH versus OOSH versions, in that this change predicts the impact of the processor-memory speed gap trend:

- the OOSH version of Barnes-Hut slows down by 3.3% when the cache miss cost is doubled, whereas making the same change in the simulation slows down the SPLASH version by 18%

- for MP3D, the difference is even bigger: the OOSH version is slowed down by 12%, whereas the SPLASH version is slowed down by 49% after doubling the simulated miss cost

MP3D is the only application measured which benefits from object blocking; since a relatively small number of repeated references is involved, the blocking gain is small. However, it is measurable, and evidence of relatively low conflict misses indicates that object blocking is a worthwhile optimization to pursue where it is applicable.

In summary, this work demonstrates that a reasonably structured, disciplined style of code using an object-oriented library is not an obstacle to competitive performance. In fact, such a style of code can make it easier to achieve good performance on new architectures, in that low-level machine-specific code should be easier to rewrite and reuse. Finally, the research shows that future generation architectures will require close attention to a programming style sympathetic to memory hierarchy issues.

1.7 Structure

The next chapter outlines characteristics of the machine architecture at which this research is targeted. The Mint simulator, used to measure performance, is also described, in the context of real machines that are surveyed in the chapter. The major purpose of Chapter 2 is to make it clear why addressing the processor-memory speed gap is likely to become increasingly important.

Other work that addresses programming the target architectures is compared with this research in Chapter 3, to complete setting the stage. The related work is presented to justify the use of an object-oriented library as a strategy for addressing the goals of the research.

The fourth chapter describes the OOSH C++ library, including key design decisions. The description is presented in sufficient detail to understand key aspects of the library's architecture.

Chapter 5 justifies the choice of applications more fully, with more detail of each application and any relevant history which helps to explain the choice of application, or which aspects of it are most relevant to this research.

Chapter 6 describes the structure of each application as implemented on top of OOSH and contrasts each implementation with its SPLASH implementation.

Chapter 7 summarizes and analyses performance results.

Finally, conclusions are presented in Chapter 8, with results evaluated against aims of the research. Opportunities for future work are also discussed in the concluding chapter.

Commentary

Since 1996, the CPU-memory speed gap has grown to the extent that further pursuit of uniprocessor speed improvement has hit a wall. While this "memory wall was predicted [Wulf and McKee 1995] in 1995 (while I was writing the thesis), the moment of reckoning was put off by increasing cache sizes, and tricks like non-blocking caches. Chip multiprocessors (now called multicore designs) became the alternative [Olukotun et al. 1996] – putting some of the ideas in this thesis into the mainstream.

Do multicore designs do away with the issues of this thesis? No. The CPU-DRAM speed gap is even bigger now than in 1996 – even with a slowdown in the aggression of the design of each core. While some aspects may be better than was possible with multichip designs (e.g, communication between processors through an on-chip bus or shared on-chip cache), unnecessary communication is still potentially a bottleneck.

References

WA Wulf and SA McKee. Hitting the Memory Wall: Implications of the Obvious, Computer Architecture News, vol. 23 no. 1, March 1995, pp 20-24

K Olukotun and BA Nayfeh and L Hammond and K Wilson and K Chang, The case for a single-chip multiprocessor, ASPLOS-VII: Proc. 7th Int. Conf. on Architectural Support for Programming Languages and Operating Systems, Cambridge, MA, 1996, pp 2-11

2. Target Architectures

2.1 Introduction

There is a growing range of commercial shared-memory multiprocessor machines, which use commodity microprocessors. The high end of this market may sometimes use processors that are not used for cheaper desktop systems, but they are generally still software-compatible with lower-end systems.

Consequently, development tools for such systems are reasonably freely obtainable. Of most interest for this research, such systems generally have C++ compilers, reasonable debugging tools, and support user-level multiprocessor applications. It is therefore feasible to write a C++ library aimed at this broad range of machines, if care is taken to isolate machine-dependent code to a small module.

Even more important in terms of the goals of this research, these systems rely on large caches, and relatively low numbers of cache misses to achieve good performance.

Since this research is attempting to address a technology trend, it is useful to survey not only high-end commercially available systems, but also research systems that hint at directions which are likely to be pursued in future commercial designs. Other similar projects indicate other possibilities for future large-scale system design; it is useful to survey these to examine the extent to which they support the underlying assumptions behind the research, especially the growing importance of cache sensitivity in software implementation.

To fully understand the reasons for the growing processor-memory speed gap, it is useful to examine the technology trends which are driving it. Understanding these trends also helps to understand trends in large-scale system design.

Once features of existing and potential future machines are understood, it becomes possible to consider a measurement strategy, which can be used to predict the impact of trends in the industry on application performance. This measurement strategy can then be used to evaluate the OOSH library, in terms of how well it reduces the impact of the growing processor-memory speed gap.

The next section of this chapter presents an overview of currently available hardware. Section 2.3 surveys research on future generation systems, with emphasis on systems scalable to a large number of processors. Section 2.4 goes on to present a summary of trends which are likely to influence future designs. This is followed by a description of the memory system simulation used for measurement in section 2.5, based on the Mint architecture simulator.

The chapter concludes with a discussion in section 2.6 of implications of the trends — identified in section 2.4 — for application design.

2.2 Commercially Available Systems

All the systems described here have major features in common. They have fast floating-point performance, which is potentially in the supercomputer league in high-end multiprocessor configurations. However, they rely on efficient use of caches to approach their theoretical peak performance, as they do not have the expensive memory systems of a traditional supercomputer, which may have hundreds of banks of RAM [Fatoohi 1990; Simmons *et al.* 1992].

Some detailed figures are supplied to help put the research (especially simulated architectures presented in the chapter on performance results) into perspective.

When reading these figures, it is useful to note that a fast DRAM at the time of writing had an access time of 60ns; a fast clock cycle time of the same era is about 200MHz, or 5ns. To make things more complicated, an increasing number of processor designs are *superscalar* (more than one instruction can be *issued* at once: an instruction is issued when it moves from the decode stage of a pipeline to the execute stage [Hennessy and Patterson 1995]), making it problematic to use clock cycle time as a measure of rate of execution.

In a multiprocessor design, it is also usually true that a bus's peak rate is not available to all processors at once, so the actual cache miss cost is also a function of bus utilization.

A final point to note before going onto specific designs is that buses and memory systems have become relatively complex in an effort at disguising the growing processor-memory speed gap, with techniques such as pipelined buses, multiple banks of RAM and large second-level (L2) caches becoming commonplace on systems such as those surveyed in this section.

Silicon Graphics has been making shared memory multiprocessor systems since the 1980s. Its Challenge range includes models with the R4400SC processor that is also used in desktop systems, and the R8000, which is intended for high-end floating point-oriented systems. The major difference between the R4400 and the R8000 is that the R8000 is a superscalar architecture, with much faster floating point performance. With a clock speed of only 75MHz, an R8000 system is rated at 300MFLOPS peak [Hsu 1994], which is much faster floating point performance than even a 200MHz R4400.

To support large-scale traditional supercomputer applications, the R8000 has support for large caches and has a relatively large TLB (translation lookaside buffer, storing recent page translations) with 384 entries [MIPS 1994]. The current range of Silicon Graphics Challenge multiprocessor systems have a 1.2Gbyte/s bus, and a minimum of 1Mbyte of second-level cache per processor. Bus bandwidth is obtained in part by a relatively wide bus: 256 bits for data and 40 for addresses. Memory can be up to 8-way interleaved, and 128 bytes are transferred to the L2 cache at a time. Maximum configuration of RAM is 16 Gbytes; there can be up to 36 R4400 CPUs or 18 R8000 processors [Galles and Williams 1994].

The peak execution rate of 300MFLOPS of the 75MHz R8000 equates to an average of one floating point operation every 3.3ns. In other words, the memory cycle time is approximately twenty times slower than the peak instruction throughput rate of the R8000. Such a crude ratio between memory and processor speed does not directly translate into cache miss cost, as factors such as cache block size, and cache controller and bus overhead also have to be taken into account. In addition, the actual cost of the memory transaction depends on how wide the bus is, and how many banks of RAM there are—both of which factors impact the number of actual full memory cycles needed for a given operation. Finally, in a superscalar design, there is a bigger variance between the best-case and worst-case instruction issue rate than with an ordinary pipeline, so it is not meaningful to give a single ratio of instruction to memory speed.

Appendix D contains a detailed calculation of read miss cost, in which it is explained how the Challenge POWERpath-2 bus can deliver a 128byte cache line from RAM in about 1μs, so the miss cost from the L2 cache is approximately 300 times slower than the fastest instruction throughput rate of a 75MHz R8000 (or 360 times slower than the more recent 90MHz model)[*]. The miss cost is typical of other similar architectures, as all work with the same underlying memory technology. This should be compared with the L2 cache miss cost of a Silicon Graphics 4D/380 system of the late 1980s. Using a simple program which times memory accesses, the L2 miss cost of the 4D/380 has been measured to be about 30 clock cycles—also about 1μs.

The relative cost of a cache miss has increased by a factor of over 10 in approximately 6 years between the two generations of Silicon Graphics multiprocessor. This order of magnitude increase in miss cost does not contradict the prediction that it takes 6.2 years for the cost of memory access to double in terms of clock cycles [Boland and Dollas 1994]: there have been other changes in the memory system in the newer design, including doubling the cache block size from 64 bytes to 128 bytes, and a change in emphasis from lowering L2 miss costs to lowering L1 miss costs (in part, the change is necessary because L2 cache sizes have increased

---

[*] Since the R8000 is a 4-way superscalar architecture, the peak throughput rate is four times the fastest rate at which a single instruction can be executed.

more than L1 cache sizes, as L1 caches have migrated from off-chip to being implemented on the CPU).

Sun has more recently moved into the realm of multiprocessor systems (using the same SPARC processors as in their uniprocessor systems), which are mainly marketed as mainframe replacements, especially in the large-scale database market. Cray builds multiprocessor compute servers, which are more scalable than Sun's models, but use the same SPARC processors as in the Sun systems.

The Cray CS6400, which uses 60MHz SuperSPARC processors, can have up to 64 processors with a maximum of 16Gbytes of RAM. High memory bandwidth is achieved by interleaving memory—with each bank attached to one of four buses—and by connecting all processors to all four buses. Each processor has a 16Kbyte first level (L1) data cache, 20Kbyte L1 instruction cache and 2Mbyte second level (L2) cache. The four buses provide a total bandwidth of 1.76Gbyte/s. The CS6400, in addition to support for multiprocessor applications, can run standard Sun software [Cray 1994].

Sun's own range of multiprocessor systems, the SPARCcenter 2000, is similar. Each processor has a 1Mbyte L2 cache, expandable to 2Mbytes. A system may be configured with 2 buses, each of which may have up to 4 banks of memory [Frailong et al. 1993]. A fully configured system can have up to 5Gbytes of RAM. The buses each have a data throughput of 320Mbyte/s. Initial models have up to 20 40MHz 3-way superscalar processors, though faster processors are supported [Cekleov et al. 1993].

The Sun and Cray models are not dissimilar in general terms from the Silicon Graphics systems, though the processors are slower. The similarity between these competing systems reinforces a major rationale for this research: systems of this nature are becoming mainstream, and work on cache-sensitive programming is potentially applicable to systems from a wide range of vendors.

To further emphasize the variety of systems available, it is useful to observe that DEC also builds a range of shared memory symmetric multiprocessor systems, including the DEC 7000 and 10000 Model 600 AXP servers. These systems were initially available with up to 6 processors though the design allows for up to 16. The 7000 uses a 182MHz Alpha 21064 processor, while the 10000 uses a 200MHz 21064. The main bus between DRAM and the CPUs is 128 bits wide with a cycle time of 20ns and usable bandwidth of 640Mbyte/s [Allison 1993]. The DEC again is similar to the Silicon Graphics design, except the total bus bandwidth is lower (reflecting the smaller maximum number of processors).

These machines all have the advantage of being based on processor architectures used for a wide range of machines, from just above the top of the personal computer range to supercomputers. Hence, the market for software—including programming tools—is larger than it would be if they were solely aimed at the high-end computation market. It is economically viable to use a wide range of configurations, from small desktop units to large supercomputer-class multiprocessor systems—depending on the scale of the problem and available funding. Consequently—for purposes of this research—they all have suitable programming tools including a C++ compiler. Also, their memory hierarchies rely on good cache behaviour and, assuming the predicted processor-memory speed gap, will increasingly require closer attention to cache behaviour to achieve good performance, as new faster processors become available.

The Kendall Square Research (KSR) architecture is a somewhat different design [Ramanathan and Oren 1993]. The KSR memory is hierarchical, with significantly higher miss cost for data further from a processor. KSR is an example of a cache-only architecture—there is no "home" location for a specific piece of data.

Unlike the other architectures in this brief survey, KSR uses a proprietary processor. A consequence is that the uniprocessor performance of a KSR machine is not very competitive. The designers claimed that low uniprocessor performance is compensated for by the architecture's scalability. However, this approach means that only relatively large and therefore expensive configurations are viable.

KSR announced in September 1994 that they were ceasing production, illustrating the difficulty of selling a machine with a relatively narrow appeal. It is possible, though, that KSR did not go out of the computation server business solely for this reason, as the company had run into some difficulties arising out of its accounting practices [Snell 1994].

In summary, at the time of writing, a competitive shared-memory multiprocessor system has memory bus bandwidth roughly of the order of 1Gbyte/s, can support several Gbytes of RAM, has at least 1Mbyte of second-level cache per processor and has up to 8 banks of interleaved RAM. These characteristics—with currently available processors—translate to an L2 cache miss cost of the order of 100 cycles (or 100 times slower than the peak execution rate for a superscalar architecture).

Systems with future processors are likely to have an even higher miss costs, given the processor-memory speed gap trend.

The number of processors supported in models reported here ranges from 6 to 64, with systems with faster processors tending to have a lower upper limit on the number of processors. Systems with still higher numbers of processors generally need more complex interconnects than a shared bus, as is described in the following section.

2.3 Research Systems

There is a number of research projects mainly aimed at making shared-memory multiprocessor systems which are more scalable than the typical commercially available systems.

Bus-based systems seldom scale to more than 40 processors—even fewer if the processors are fast. The systems surveyed in this section are designed to scale to hundreds of processors. Most of these research systems tackle the problem of scaling up a bus-based architecture by splitting the bus into some kind of hierarchy.

These systems are of significance for this research, because they are also sensitive to poor cache behaviour—and because they represent the possibility of building higher-performance systems than those surveyed in the previous section, if the issue of cache behaviour can be addressed.

ParaDiGM is one of two projects at Stanford University. ParaDiGM has a hierarchy of buses and caches. Processors are grouped in clusters, with each cluster sharing an L2 cache. The next level down can also be grouped into clusters, resulting

processors are relatively slow in the company of the recent commercial systems surveyed in the previous section should be taken into account. The Alewife processors are modified SPARC processors, running at 33MHz [Chaiken *et al.* 1991]. If the architecture were implemented with more competitive processors, it is likely that it would also become sensitive to a high number of invalidations.

Overall, these architectures demonstrate that scaling shared memory beyond the capabilities of buses makes reducing misses even more important. Misses over a network or down a hierarchy are significantly more expensive than misses on a single bus. Achieving the goals of this research therefore will become even more useful should architectures such as these surveyed in this section become common.

2.4 Technology Trends

Since the advent of commercial RISC (reduced instruction set computer) architectures in the mid-1980s, the speed improvement of new microprocessors has been in the range 50% to 100% per year (see figure 2.1). On the other hand, DRAM speed improvement over the same period has been approximately 7% per year [Hennessy and Patterson 1995]. On average, in recent years, it has taken 6.2 years for the cost of memory access in clock cycles to double [Boland and Dollas 1994].

As a consequence of these trends, caches are becoming increasingly important for high processor performance. Most current high performance systems have at least two levels of cache.

On-chip first-level (L1) caches in microprocessors on sale in 1995 generally vary from 4Kbytes to 16Kbytes for each of instruction and data caches (mostly

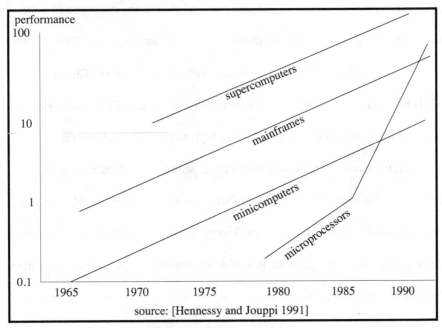

Figure 2.1 CPU Performance Trends

separate though the IBM PowerPC 601 has a combined 32Kbyte L1 cache).

A second level (L2) cache of 1Mbyte is almost commonplace, and high end systems in 1994 have as much as 4Mbytes of L2 cache.

At least for the next 5 years it seems likely that these trends will continue, or if anything be accentuated. The difficulty in speeding up DRAM is a consequence of the economics of the memory market. The DRAM market is driven by cost, which drives density up (an average of a factor of four every three years [Hennessy and Patterson 1995]). At the same time, the underlying technology of DRAM—in which a read is performed by draining the charge on a capacitor, which must subsequently be recharged—is not only inherently slow [Prince 1994], but becomes is harder to make fast as the capacitor is shrunk (and therefore capable of holding less charge).

With static RAM, the driving force in the market is both cost and speed [Hennessy and Patterson 1995]. An SRAM stores bits in flip-flops constructed out of transistors, which are designed to be ready to read immediately after a read operation [Prince 1994].

Another factor in the rapid acceleration of CPU performance is the gains to be had from higher component counts which allow more parallelism in the execution path [Hennessy and Jouppi 1991].

A similar performance gain to that seen in processors is harder to realize at low cost with DRAM, though there are attempts at disguising some of the latency of DRAM by methods such as incorporating a cache on the DRAM chip, or using a very fast bus to transfer a large number of bytes in a stream. Rambus for example does both [Farmwald and Mooring 1992].

In a limited sense, the relationship between DRAM and the processor can be seen to be moving closer to the long-standing relationship between DRAM and disk.

With current miss costs, page faults are handled in software to allow more sophisticated strategies which reduce the number of misses, whereas cache misses are handled in hardware to minimize latency of each miss.

In the long term, it may be desirable to go for more expensive but more intelligent cache management strategies. Some have been advocating software cache management for a number of years [Cheriton *et al.* 1986]. Others have predicted that faster clock cycle times will soon result in cache miss costs of hundreds of cycles [Jouppi 1990], which could make software miss handling viable. Manufacturers are using increasingly sophisticated strategies, including wider buses, interleaved memory and bigger caches [MIPS 1994; Galles and Williams 1994; Cray 1994] to avoid the need for more sophisticated (and therefore software implemented) cache management. Despite these improvements, however, as is shown in section 2.2, cache miss costs of the order of 100 instructions or more are indeed becoming common. Software miss handling is not a feature of any of the real systems surveyed here, but experience with Alewife [Chaiken *et al.* 1991] suggests that software miss handling may have benefits for new architectures, especially in large scalable systems with a slower interconnect than a shared bus.

A final point of significance to this research is that cache block sizes are likely to increase to attempt to amortize the cost of misses (i.e., to achieve a larger prefetch effect). A technology such as Rambus, which transfers units of 512 bytes at a time, is suited to transferring large blocks. However, a larger prefetch unit also means more false sharing in a shared-memory multiprocessor system.

2.5 Mint

The difficulty of obtaining repeatable measures on a real machine is a major advantage of using an architecture simulator. In addition, a simulator allows for measurements that would be difficult on real hardware, such as the number and cause of cache misses.

For taking measurements of memory hierarchies, two major categories of simulator are useful: trace-driven and direct execution simulators. A memory trace is a record of addresses referenced on one specific run, which may be run through a simulator multiple times, with different parameters (such as memory access costs), to simulate different memory hierarchies. A direct execution simulator on the other hand directly executes the code every time, using software emulation where necessary to allow simulation of new features of a proposed architecture.

There has been work on efficient tracing systems [Larus 1993], but given the potential for introducing subtle inaccuracies when using traces to simulate different memory systems [Koldinger *et al.* 1991], a direct architecture simulator is preferable, if its performance is acceptable.

The Mint (MIPS Interpreter) architecture simulator [Veenstra 1993] provides a comprehensive simulation of the MIPS R3000 instruction set, and most of the R4000 instruction set, and can be used for either kind of simulation. Mint reduces the overhead of simulation by executing parts of basic blocks that do not do loads or stores (and hence do not have data references, since MIPS is a load-store architecture) directly. Only branch and memory reference instructions are actually simulated. Another advantage of Mint is that it uses its own lightweight process implementation to efficiently simulate multiprocessor runs.

Tango [Goldschmidt and Davis 1990] can also be used for either trace-driven or direct execution simulation. In some respects, it is less efficiently implemented than Mint. Mint allows standard object code to be executed directly on the simulator, whereas Tango requires recompiling the source with an extra augmentation step. Tango also has a less efficient model of multitasking (using UNIX processes), and is generally slower than Mint. Tango-lite has since been developed, which addresses most of the problems raised here, but was not available in time to be considered.

For these reasons, Mint is used for simulations reported here, though Tango has been used in earlier work [Cheriton *et al*. 1991b].

The Mint simulator backend can be partially or completely rewritten depending on the sophistication of the required memory system simulation. In the default case, the backend does nothing, and running under Mint does little more than collect a few global statistics. With empty backend functions, Mint is claimed to run between 18 and 65 times slower than native execution for a uniprocessor run [Veenstra 1993].

The backend used for this research is based on an example supplied with Mint, which implements a simple infinite cache model. Additions have been made to the supplied code to generate more statistics and to simulate miss costs more realistically. In particular, the bus has been modified to more closely approximate that of a current design in terms of memory access costs. A finite cache simulator has also been written, based on the infinite cache code, to measure blocking effects. More detail of the simulators is presented in Appendix B.

The simulation is run with a miss cost of 50 processor cycles, as well as with double the miss cost (100 cycles), to measure the impact of trends in CPU versus memory speed. The higher figure has already been exceeded by high-end systems, and even higher miss costs will become commonplace as current high-end processors move down the scale.

The trend of a doubling of DRAM cost in processor cycles every 6.2 years [Boland and Dollas 1994] puts the two simulated memory systems about 6 years apart — though this is a simplistic assumption, as details of the memory system other than access time, such as cache block size, affect miss cost. Alternatively, the two variations can be seen as representing a high end and a low end system (respectively, either fast or slow processors on the same memory system).

An infinite cache model is suitable to measure shared memory communication costs, which may be obscured by capacity or conflict misses in a finite cache simulation; a finite cache simulation is necessary to measure blocking effects, since blocking mainly aims to reduce capacity misses.

Specifics of the parameters of the simulation are given in section 7.2, where the measurement strategy is described. The simulated architecture is described in more detail in Appendix B.

2.6 Implications of Architecture Trends For Applications

It is becoming increasingly difficult to avoid the need to do at least some restructuring of applications, as cache block sizes and cache miss penalties increase.

If software is written in an object-oriented style, it is possible to replace low-level memory allocators to ensure that objects are padded and aligned to cache blocks. If data is allocated in an ad hoc fashion or in arrays this is harder to achieve.

False sharing is not a major problem with small cache blocks. Provided that blocks are smaller than most data structures, no special effort is needed to avoid having blocks containing unrelated data. In the limit, if blocks are the size of the smallest data structure, there is no false sharing. On the other hand, as the size of cache blocks increases, the probability of false sharing increases.

For relatively large data structures, or those that do not occur often, padding and alignment is viable. For smaller frequently occurring data structures, the cost in lost memory makes it preferable to aggregate multiple smaller data structures that are assigned to the same processor.

The same kind of issue is likely to be encountered for a wide range of software, so it would be useful to be able to reuse code that implements solutions to these problems. Since one of the goals of object-oriented programming is the promotion of code reuse [Cox 1991], developing an object-oriented library such as OOSH is an appropriate strategy. Chapter 3 justifies the implementation strategy more fully, by comparing it with related work.

Commentary

It is tempting to sneer at the weird and wonderful architectures around in that era, most of which did not survive. However, there is some pretty weird stuff around now, which strikes me as unlikely to go anywhere. One example is the Sony-Toshiba-IBM Cell architecture, which repeats all the lessons of how not to design a parallel machine in one go: it has user-programmable local memory, a specialized vector instruction set, an inhomogeneous architecture and no clear and obvious programming model.

The mainstream parallel architecture was established already in the 1990s: symmetric shared-memory – for one very good reason. It has a sane programming model. Other variants like the Cell and general-purpose programming of graphics processors are only now re-arising because they have a specialist market which is huge, creating a temptation to push them to greater generality. I'll believe it when I stop seeing PhD theses around writing one program on them.

The whole Cell thing would have been a lot more plausible had Sony's Playstation 3 launched with a significant number of games using all the features of Cell. It didn't. If something with so much riding on it commercially – being the first to produce a cool game on new platform – couldn't make good use of it, you have to conclude that there isn't a sane programming model for it.

3.   Related Work

3.1 Introduction

This chapter places the research in context. In particular, the reasons for choosing to implement an object-oriented library are clarified, by examining other strategies for implementing efficient shared-memory parallel code.

Work most closely related to that reported on here is attempts at implementing object-oriented languages and macro packages for shared-memory multiprocessor programs. Work on implementing algorithms efficiently on shared-memory systems is also closely related, as is work on automatic optimization (or even automatic parallelization) in the field of compiler research—though much work on compiler optimization turns out to be inapplicable to C++.

Less closely related is work on alternative synchronization mechanisms. The major focus in this work is on using C++ features to best effect, to minimize communication costs—especially by reducing sharing. Ideally, all false sharing should be eliminated, and true sharing should be minimized. A limited investigation has been made of alternative methods of synchronization as part of the research, to demonstrate that the generality of the OOSH library—rather than to pursue a goal of exploring the space of alternative synchronization constructs.

Since some of the work done by others on synchronization could be adapted to OOSH, it is described in more detail in this chapter than is justified by the major goals of the research. The purpose of this presentation is to illustrate that a library such as OOSH can provide a basis for implementing the features expected of a parallel programming language.

The next section of this chapter contains a brief overview of features of the OOSH library, which summarizes the overview of section 1.5 in the form of pointers to the related work covered in the rest of this chapter. Presentation of detail of the library is deferred to Chapter 4.

Section 3.3 presents algorithmic and compiler methods to reduce cache misses; these two techniques are handled together, since compiler optimizations may also be manually implemented. Section 3.4 contains a brief survey of object-oriented approaches to implementing shared-memory programming constructs (libraries and languages), followed by a summary of approaches to implementing synchronization efficiently in section 3.5.

In conclusion, in section 3.6, related work is compared with this research and the strategy of building an object-oriented library is further justified.

3.2 How OOSH Relates to Other Work

The OOSH library design is based on two major strategies: spatial decomposition, and cache block-sensitive memory allocators.

Spatial decomposition should be compared with related work which supports *processor affinity* scheduling (see COOL in section 3.4.2), as well as related work on *blocking* (in section 3.3). Work on reducing false sharing (also covered in section

3.3) should be compared with the OOSH approach of implementing cache-sensitive memory allocators.

Although the major goal of the OOSH library is to support efficient memory referencing patterns, some work has been put into design of a new synchronization strategy called *distributed synchronization*. Distributed synchronization should be compared with techniques in section 3.5 for reducing cache misses associated with synchronization operations.

In terms of programming technique, the approach of using a constructor and destructor to implement locks should be compared with a similar strategy that has been used in PRESTO, which is described in section 3.4.

3.3 Algorithmic Strategies and Compiler Optimizations

There is a major attraction to finding compiler optimizations to reduce cache misses. If such optimizations are effective for popular languages, a large body of *legacy* code (programs which have been in use for a long time, which may have become unmaintainable: also known as *dusty decks*) can be run efficiently without modification.

In the realm of large-scale numeric computation, much such code is written in FORTRAN. Partially for this reason, much of the work on memory-related optimization in compilers for high-performance computation has been done for FORTRAN. Another reason for the emphasis on FORTRAN in compiler work is that many of the techniques used assume there are no *aliases* (more than one variable that refers to the same place in memory). FORTRAN code can contain aliases (e.g.

through the EQUIVALENCE statement, or through parameter passing), but the need for aliases is much lower than in languages with pointers and dynamic allocation. It is therefore acceptable for an optimizing compiler to require that there are no aliases in a FORTRAN program — if there are any, they are considered to be a bug [Bacon *et al.* 1994].

Even if many of the transformations performed by a compiler cannot be safely done automatically in the presence of aliases, it is possible in principle to use these techniques manually. For example, *blocking* (also called *tiling*) is the strategy of doing as much computation as possible on a subset of the data set that fits into a cache, before moving on to other data*. Blocking is often worth implementing even if the compiler does not support it. One complication that arises in implementing blocking is choosing a block size that minimizes conflict misses (where different addresses map to the same cache block) [Lam *et al.* 1991].

Blocking is most likely to be of benefit in applications that share a major characteristic of algorithms such as a matrix multiply: the same data is referenced in many different places. In the case of multiplying two *N*x*N* matrices, for example, a specific element of one of the arrays is used in *N* different computations.

Another transformation which is potentially possible for a compiler to implement, but which is also implemented manually by shared-memory programmers, is *block decomposition*: chunking an array into units that are aligned to cache blocks [Bacon *et al.* 1994]. For example, if the block size is 32 bytes and an

---

* Blocking was originally proposed for uniprocessor computations.

array element is 4 bytes, the smallest unit of the array allocated to one processor is 8 elements, with the divisions chosen so that they fall on cache block boundaries. The MP3D program in the SPLASH benchmarks [Singh *et al.* 1992b], for example, is implemented in this way.

On the other hand, attempting to implement object-oriented code on a high-performance system without attempting to do manual optimizations may yield disappointing results [Forslund *at al.* 1990].

Many of the optimizations that are applicable to parallel machines are also applicable to uniprocessor systems, though contention in the multiprocessor case for shared resources adds additional problems, such as false sharing.

The following is a partial list of relevant techniques in addition to those already described, to give an idea of what can be done [Bacon *et al.* 1994]:

- *loop reordering* — may expose parallelism: useful especially for automatic parallelizers, but also can be used to avoid bank conflicts in a uniprocessor or vector system with multiple banks of RAM

- *array padding* — moving the start of an array — can reduce memory bank, or cache set or TLB set conflicts on uniprocessor systems; it can also be used to address false sharing on shared-memory systems

- *cache alignment* — strategies such as ensuring that a shared variable and the associated lock go in the same cache block can reduce false sharing

All of these techniques are potentially possible to implement in a compiler, especially for a language like FORTRAN where aliases may be disallowed.

However, for those who wish to switch to an object-oriented language such as C++, much research is still needed to find ways of implementing these strategies automatically. In the meantime, performing such optimizations manually is possible.

3.4 Object-Oriented Shared-Memory Languages and Libraries

This section is split into two parts: C++ class libraries, and special-purpose parallel languages. Rather than an exhaustive coverage of such alternatives, this section aims to present a representative sample, to make it clearer where the OOSH library fits into the range of possibilities.

3.4.1 C++ Libraries

The ANL Parmacs macros have been translated into a C++ class library [Beck 1990]. The C++ Parmacs library re-implements the major functionality of the macros including monitors, barriers and distributed index generators. The library uses classes to implement each feature, and inheritance is used to build features up out of primitives, as well as to demonstrate the development of new features based on those similar to the original macros. Despite the improvements over the original macros, the C++ version of Parmacs does not address the major issue of this research: efficient use of caches.

The PRESTO threads package, developed at the University of Washington [Bershad *et al.* 1988], is one of the earlier attempts at building a shared-memory multiprocessing toolkit in C++. PRESTO pioneered some useful techniques, such as using constructors and destructors to set up and terminate a parallel programming construct. For example, this is how PRESTO monitors are implemented.

PRESTO differs in emphasis from the work of this thesis in that it addresses issues of efficient implementation of low-level primitives like locks, monitors and thread management. The OOSH implementation assumes that building efficient primitives is addressed by other research, and from this starting point provides a framework for a specific class of applications. In another difference in emphasis, PRESTO does not address the issue of program structuring to reduce cache misses.

3.4.2 Parallel Object-Based and Object-Oriented Languages

The COOL language developed at Stanford is an extension of C++ with features like class-based monitors, affinity hints to encourage scheduling of related processes on the same processor, parallel functions and a range of synchronization operations.

Although COOL aims to reduce memory costs by improving processor affinity, it does not include allocators for aligned, padded objects. Improvement in processor affinity is a useful goal, but some work on application structure is also necessary to ensure that the application has reasonable locality. Since COOL is a programming language rather than an application framework, it does not address program structure.

Also, although COOL is a preprocessor-based extension to C++, it does not support full use of the language for parallel constructs: inheritance is not supported [Wyatt et al. 1992]. It is therefore more correctly described as an *object-based* (as opposed to object-oriented) language [Booch 1991], since inheritance is a fundamental requirement of a true object-oriented language [Cardelli and Wegner 1985].

COOL has a much longer feature list than OOSH. Applications reported on in published work on COOL are similar to those implemented here — if a wider range of applications and in some cases newer improved versions [Chandra *et al.* 1994]. Since COOL has more features than OOSH, it could prove to be more generally applicable. However, in principle, the functionality of OOSH could be extended as needed.

Most other object-oriented languages or object-based with support for parallelism predate concerns for efficient use of memory hierarchy. Some of these languages include Concurrent Smalltalk, Eiffel [Wyatt *et al.* 1992] and Ada [DoD 1983].

3.5 Synchronization Strategies

This section presents a few possibilities for synchronization, to illustrate possibilities for future work. Strategies that are relevant to shared-memory programming could be incorporated into the library. However, since the focus of the research is reducing cache misses, relatively simple approaches to synchronization were generally considered sufficient for OOSH. However, where restructuring can reduce the need for synchronization, such restructuring is worth considering — see for example the *distributed synchronization* strategy adopted for MP3D in 6.2.2.

Most work on novel strategies for synchronization has been done for distributed memory systems, since communication costs on these systems are high. Also, on a distributed memory system, it is not possible for a processor to look into another's address space, so problems like deadlock detection are more of an issue than for shared-memory systems.

As latencies for memory access increase, it is possible that shared memory systems will require some of the strategies used in distributed memory systems. Some of the work by others aimed at distributed memory systems includes *virtual time* and *distributed mutual exclusion*.

Virtual time is based on the idea that a process may *optimistically* assume that it has not moved ahead of other parts of a simulation. If, however, it receives a message from another part of the simulation that is older than work the process has already completed, the process must *roll back* work to the time of the newly received message, and broadcast *antimessages* to inform other processes that they must roll back work resulting from any now invalidated messages originating from the rolling back process [Fujimoto 1990].

Virtual time, or the optimistic simulation model, is most suited to cases where the amount of memory used by a simulation is relatively small in relation to the amount of processing required. Also, the communication cost for checking clocks of other parts of a simulation must be high in relation to potential losses from broadcasting anti-messages and performing a rollback. In current shared-memory systems, these limitations restrict the class of applicable applications more than on distributed memory systems, or distributed systems (i.e., optimistic simulation is less attractive on a shared-memory system).

Distributed mutual exclusion is intended mainly for distributed systems, but is applicable to any system connected by a network, including a distributed shared memory system. Mutual exclusion is necessary for managing any shared resource, including atomic file transactions. Fault tolerance is a major requirement of the general solution to distributed mutual exclusion, since a networked distributed system can include networked nodes which may go down, and parts of the network itself may fail [Agrawal and El Abbadi 1991].

While fault tolerance is not as important to programmers of shared memory systems, some of the issues that arise in achieving efficient implementation of distributed mutual exclusion may become relevant as memory latencies rise in relation to CPU speeds.

Research on synchronization for shared-memory systems has focused more on improving the speed of existing mechanisms than on finding novel mechanisms.

For example, tree-based barriers solve essentially the same problem as the distributed synchronization strategy introduced by this research, but without requiring any change to program structure [Mellor-Crumney and Scott 1991].

Cache coherency-based locks are implemented as part of the cache mechanism. Instead of using lock variables and relying on the usual cache coherency protocol to ensure atomicity of an attempt at acquiring a lock, the cache controller implements the lock mechanism. Cache coherency-based locks address the problem of hot spots caused by locks [Cheriton *et al*. 1991a].

Contention-free locks attempt to solve the lock hot spot problem without special hardware. For example, a ticket lock gives a process attempting to acquire a lock a number. When the global lock value reaches the value of the process's ticket, it has acquired the lock. It only sets the global value on releasing the lock. The number of invalidations can be minimized by using two different counters for picking up the ticket and for the global count that is tested. This is an improvement on a test-and-set lock where every processor attempting to acquire the lock spins on it and attempts to set it constantly (conditional on its value), and also a little more efficient that a test-and-test-and-set lock, where every process waiting on the lock only tries to set it when its value changes [Mellor-Crumney and Scott 1991].

Distributed shared memory systems are making increased use of relaxed consistency models, such as *release consistency*, in which it is assumed that shared variables will only be written when shared by a lock. In the release consistency model, dirty blocks only need be written back when a lock is released. To ensure atomicity of the write, the release is blocked until the write back is complete [Dwarkadas *et al*. 1993]. Release consistency is also used in the DASH architecture, which is not a distributed shared memory system but does have high latency for misses far down the hierarchy [Lenoski *et al*. 1992].

Adopting such relaxed consistency models, while a memory system implementation technique, cannot be considered in isolation from strategies for synchronization since it relies on the interaction between memory referencing and locking.

3.6 Conclusion

When comparing strategies for implementing new approaches to programming, it is useful to distinguish between improving existing code and writing new code. For improving existing code, it is hard to argue against compiler optimization work, since legacy code can be improved without having to understand it in detail.

However, the difficulties of generalizing some important compiler optimizations to languages with unrestricted pointers makes it difficult to implement many optimizations that can be applied to FORTRAN to a language such as C++. Another drawback of relying on compiler optimizations is that all code has to be recompiled if a new optimization is found. If a new optimization is implemented by changing a library however, at worst only relinking is needed (many systems today support dynamic libraries, so even relinking may not be needed).

When completely new code is to be written, it is more feasible to consider other alternatives—such as using a new language.

For writing new code, implementing features such as efficient reusable memory allocators and synchronization primitives in a library using standard C++ has some advantages over inventing a new language, whether by using a macro processor to extend an existing language or by implementing a totally new language.

Portability is easier to achieve with a library than with a completely new language. Portability may to some extent be addressed by implementing the language using a macro processor to translate it to a standard language. However, debugging code that has been passed through a macro processor can become difficult. Even though UNIX-based tools allow such extra levels of translation to be hidden to some extent, it is always possible that problems will lead to a need to examine the translated code.

Furthermore, improvements (such as new synchronization strategies or better memory allocators) are relatively easy to add to a library.

As latencies for memory systems increase, strategies similar to release consistency will become increasingly common, and new programming methods will have to take such models of consistency into account. A library-based approach in which low level hardware-dependent allocators are hidden from the user can be modified for such new strategies.

Whenever such improvements are made, the library will be altered. As long as the programming model is unchanged, programs using the library should only need to be relinked. If a shared library is used, even linking may not be necessary.

A programming language that hides details of parallel coding from the programmer also runs into the problem of requiring recompilation of existing code to obtain the benefits of the new approach. Worse, changing a language primitive may require rewriting the compiler—or at least the runtime library.

In the best case, making improvements to the implementation of a programming language may be restricted to rewriting parts of the run-time library. However, if this is true, much of the functionality supplied in the language would have to be contained in the library routines, so it becomes less clear that implementing a new language is what is required. If the same effect can be obtained by implementing a library without implementing a special-purpose language, the library-only strategy should be the more economical solution in terms of effort to implement.

In summary, OOSH addresses the issues of efficient structuring by spatial decomposition of applications (with potential for object blocking), as well as allocating memory aligned and padded to cache block boundaries, unlike most of the other work surveyed here. A library is in some respects a more efficient strategy than compiler optimizations, though compiler optimizations would be useful if they could be extended to languages that allow unrestricted use of pointers. One advantage though of using a library instead of relying on compiler optimizations is that improvements can be made without recompiling anything but the library. A library is easier to modify for new synchronization or memory management strategies than a language such as COOL; strategies such as tree-based barriers could be added (for example) with no change to applications built with the library. With dynamic shared libraries, the possibility is created to vary the strategy transparently across a family of machines, or to install new binaries of a new release without requiring recompilation.

Commentary

Although specific products mentioned here may not be current, the principle of implementation in libraries (or APIs) rather than in languages remains good. Java for example implements threads, but most other languages in common use have kept parallelism out of the language.

4.   The OOSH C++ Library

4.1 Introduction

This chapter explains the key design decisions of the OOSH library. It is not intended as complete documentation of the library's functionality, but is intended to convey sufficient detail to understand major aspects of the library's architecture.

The purpose of this chapter is to demonstrate the suitability of features of C++ for implementation of parallel programming constructs, with the goal of supporting a cache-sensitive style of programming in a reusable way.

"Cache-sensitive" here is taken to mean support for spatial decomposition of programs — including object-blocking — and padding and alignment to cache block boundaries. "Reusable" is taken to mean that a large part of the lower-level functionality, including padded and aligned memory allocators and parallel-programming primitives need not be reimplemented for each application.

These are subjective issues, and since the main focus of the research is to measure performance of the resulting code and predict its performance on future architectures, no attempt is made at precisely quantifying them.

Section 4.2 provides an overview of the major architectural decisions taken in the design process, divided into issues related to the simulation model, and a description of the implementation strategy. This is followed in section 4.3 by an overview of the flow of control of an application built on top of OOSH. The library is broken down into machine-dependent classes, kernel classes and higher-level classes. Each of these major sub-divisions is separately discussed, in sections 4.4 to 4.6.

After discussion of the library, construction of applications on top of the library is discussed in general terms, in section 4.7. More specific discussion of application information is contained in Chapter 6, which covers detail of how the applications implemented and measured for this research are implemented using OOSH.

4.2 Architecture

OOSH provides a starting point for implementing timestepped simulations, with support for spatial decomposition and primitives for shared memory programming, including cache-aligned and padded memory allocation, locks, barriers and process creation.

This section describes the general model of timestepped simulations that OOSH supports, followed by detail of the strategy used to implement the library.

4.2.1 Simulation Model

The model of a timestepped simulation on which OOSH is built is similar to that of a number of applications in the Stanford SPLASH benchmarks [Singh et al. 1992b]. Since timestepped simulation is a fairly general model, principles explained here are more generally applicable, but examples used here are drawn from SPLASH since it is an accepted collection of benchmarks. For the same reason, SPLASH programs are used in this research.

At the outer level, a loop iterates over timesteps, until sufficient timesteps have been executed. At each timestep, the simulation state is recomputed. In practice, this usually means that the entire data set is referenced each timestep. For a cache architecture, any data set that is larger than the cache will sweep the caches—i.e., all data is likely to be replaced at least once per timestep. Consequently, it is important to exploit any locality that may be inherent in the simulation. Ideally, data needs only be brought into the cache once per timestep if locality can be exploited to maximum benefit.

Some simulations only communicate data locally in the simulated space—which can be used to achieve good memory reference locality in an implementation. For example, in MP3D [McDonald and Baganoff 1988]—a particle-based wind tunnel simulation—particles do not move far in one timestep. Particles carry all information which moves through the simulation, so an implementation can be decomposed spatially, with the effect that data movement from one processor to another is minimized. It is also possible—as can be seen when earlier versions of MP3D are described in Chapter 6—to fail to exploit the inherent locality of the simulated space when implementing the simulation. It is important to realize that locality in the simulated space and locality in the program are different concepts; OOSH is aimed at making facilitating implementation such that simulated space locality translates to good locality in the program.

Locality in simulated space is often found in physical systems that can be modeled as kinetic particles with short mean free paths, for example. In general, physical systems can often be modeled using local interactions [Sproull and Phillips

1980]. One example of a useful application with such properties is simulation of chemical vapour deposition (CVD), which is an important step in semiconductor manufacturing [Dosanj 1995]. Another example—this time of an algorithm that may be useful for simulations, rather than a physical system—which has a kind of "space-based" locality is the successive over-relaxation method (SOR) for solving partial differential equations, which has been shown to be possible to implement efficiently on a cache-based architecture [Cheriton *et al* 1991a].

Some broad application domains in which problems may have suitable properties for the OOSH model include exploration geophysics, modelling of complex radar images and molecular dynamics. In all of these areas, communication, data structures and work allocation are irregular in space, and therefore not easy to implement efficiently using a simple array-based strategy, but communication tends to be relatively localized [Camp *et al.* 1994].

In other simulations, information may be more globally shared. For example, Barnes-Hut is an *n*-body gravitation simulation [Barnes and Hut 1986], and recomputing the effects of gravitation requires global information. In this case, a spatial decomposition strategy offers less potential for improvement than with MP3D. However, Barnes-Hut does more computation per time-step per particle (or body) than MP3D: Barnes-Hut is $O(n \log n)$ per time step, whereas MP3D is $O(n)$ per timestep.

Barnes-Hut's larger amount of computation per timestep makes it less sensitive to cache misses than MP3D, since a cache miss is amortized over more instructions. However, if the memory-processor gap continues to grow, even applications with heavy computation may benefit from closer attention to exploiting locality. In the case of Barnes-Hut, this would mean finding a new algorithm—or at very least, a new way of hierarchically organizing space (the spatial hierarchy of Barnes-Hut is described in section 5.4).

4.2.2 Architecture

There are two major strategies in implementation of reusable classes: loosely structured libraries and application frameworks.

The Smalltalk–80 class library [Goldberg and Robson 1983] is a good example of a loosely structured set of classes. The library supplies a wide range of abstract classes, container classes and classes for specific purposes such as graphics and user interfaces.

At the opposite end of the scale, application frameworks such as those becoming widely available on platforms such as Microsoft Windows and the Apple Macintosh essentially provide a starting point for writing an application, in which the major flow of control is prewritten, and derived classes have to be supplied to fill in application-specific behavior.

OOSH falls somewhere between the two extremes: although it is an application framework, it does not define much detail of the structure of an application. It has a fixed outer level flow of control once processes are launched, but very little detail is predefined. The rationale for the OOSH design compromise is that a supplied high-level order of execution makes it easier to start programming from scratch; predefining too much detail makes it harder to retrofit applications to the library.

The flow of control in its default form is designed to dispatch units of work in a spatially decomposed application. As is illustrated when application implementations are described in Chapter 6, the framework is sufficiently flexible to support other application structures.

Part of the spatial decomposition strategy is dividing work into units smaller than the cache, to facilitate blocking. A natural unit of work for the application— which would typically correspond to a subdivision of simulation space—may be suitable for this. However it may also be true that such a subdivision is too small to efficiently schedule. For this reason, simulation space is divided into schedulable units, called *precincts* and atomic units of work, called *space units*.

OOSH uses constructors and destructors extensively, following the example of PRESTO [Bershad *et al.* 1988]. Some parallel constructs need to be called in pairs, for example, launching and terminating processes, and locking and unlocking. These constructs are implemented by declaration of a variable of a class designed for this purpose. The compiler ensures that the constructor is called when the variable comes into scope, and when it goes out of scope. This is most useful as it saves the programmer from having to remember to put in the second half of the construct whenever necessary (for example, at every `return` statement). In the event that greater control is needed, the programmer still has the option of more explicitly deciding when the constructor and destructor are called by using dynamic allocation. In this case, the constructor is called when operator `new` is invoked, and the destructor when `delete` is used to deallocate the object.

OOSH classes are grouped into several logical layers, following the practice of Smalltalk–80. These layers provide an additional level of abstraction, and help the programmer to distinguish classes which are meant to be hidden from those which may be freely used. The layers are:

- *machine-dependent*—classes not meant to be seen directly in applications

- *kernel*—low-level functionality and primitives, built on the machine-dependent layer

- *higher-level*—classes which are more specific to the application architecture.

  The higher-level classes are further divided into the following groups of classes:

- *space*—division of application space into units of work and per-processor data; the smallest unit of space scheduled at once is a *precinct* (see 4.6 for more detail)

- *environment*—initialization and interpretation of command-line arguments

- *command*—optional command interpreter

  Following sections elaborate on the implementation strategy, starting with a description of control flow, after which more detail of each layer is presented.

4.3 Control Flow

Flow of control in OOSH is based on the assumption that the application has been spatially decomposed, and work is therefore allocated to each processor in the form of a queue of precincts. This section provides an overview of the outermost level of control; more detail of precincts and other aspects of spatial decomposition is provided when the higher-level classes are discussed in section 4.6.

There is no predefined synchronization between or within timesteps; it is up to a specific application to implement barriers or distributed synchronization at appropriate points in its code.

Figure 4.1 contains pseudocode for the dispatch loop which is the outermost level of control of an OOSH application—once the parallel part of the code has started. This section contains a description of the major points of the dispatch loop. Once the overall flow of control is understood, the context in which the other classes are used should become clearer.

The major classes discussed in this section are

- `Process`—contains the state needed to launch a new process, but not application-specific information; member functions include

— `dispatch` (a static member function[*]): which contains the main loop for scheduling work

- `Proc_data`—contains a queue of precincts and application-specific information which relates to a specific process; each application should derive a new class based on `Proc_data`; member functions include

— `get_load`: if the application implements dynamic load balancing, `get_load` does the necessary work (the detail is totally application-dependent: the default implementation does nothing)

---

[*] A C++ *static member function* corresponds to a class method in Smalltalk–80: it can be called without reference to a specific object.

— `step_final`: any work which a specific process must do at the end of a timestep after processing all its precincts

The outermost level of control is invoked by creating an object of class `Process`, *n* times for a run on *n* processors. Only the first *n*-1 constructors for `Process` actually create a new process, as the parent process is also used to do work. A total of *n* processes then concurrently execute the dispatch loop, contained in the static member function `Process::dispatch`. The function needs to be static so it can be passed to an operating system process creation primitive if necessary (the detail depends on the machine-specific implementation). `Process::dispatch` looks up its per-processor data (in an object of a class derived from `Proc_data`) and finds its precinct queue.

Once initialized, `dispatch` goes into a loop in which it calls `get_load` on its private data, then asks each of its precincts (see 4.6 below) to try to work. The function `get_load` by default does nothing; if an application is to do dynamic load balancing, it must define its own `get_load` in its class derived from `Proc_data`. The loop repeats until all precincts report that they have completed all their work. For applications implemented in this research, one pass over all precincts corresponds to a simulation timestep.

C++-like pseudo code for `dispatch` is given in figure 4.1.

Each of `try_to_work`, `get_load` and `step_final` have predefined defaults: the latter two default to doing nothing, and have to be defined for a specific application as needed. The default implementation of `try_to_work` (which can also be replaced) is described in section 4.6. An application can be built on the OOSH

```
Process::dispatch (Process *owner)
    Precinct *this_precinct;
    boolean more_to_do, done_work;
    Proc_data *mine = owner->get_processor_data();
    Precinct_queue * my_precincts = mine->get_precincts ();
    do
    { more_to_do = FALSE;
    done_work = FALSE;
    mine->get_load ();
    for (∀ precinct ∈ my_precincts)
        if (precinct->still_working ())
        {   more_to_do = TRUE;
            if (precinct->try_to_work (mine))
                done_work = TRUE;
        }
        mine->step_final (more_to_do);
    } while (more_to_do);
}
```

Figure 4.1 The Dispatch Loop

framework if it fits it closely—or effectively sidestep it, by doing all its work in only one or two of the get_load, try_to_work or step_final phases. These variations are illustrated in the next chapter, where implementation of specific applications is described.

OOSH is designed on the assumption that new classes will not be derived from Process. The constructor for Process launches and starts executing a new process. Since constructors of a parent (base) classes are executed first, a class derived from Process would not have its own constructor executed until after execution of the new process has terminated. If a specialization of processor-specific data or functions is required, the correct place to implement this specialization is in a class derived from Proc_data.

4.4 Machine-Dependent Classes

The innermost layer of the classes is in a machine-specific file that implements classes:

- Synch_info (internal data and code for implementing barriers)

- MP_info (determine number of processors, pin a process to a specific processor and determine page size)

- Lock_info (internal data for locks and code for locking and unlocking)

- Machine_process (launch processes, wait for other processes to terminate, allocate and clean up shared memory, report how much shared memory allocated)

- Timing (subtract another time from this, return seconds, return microseconds, set time from system clock: in UNIX, subclassed from timeval struct)

These classes are designed to be easy to implement on top of typical UNIX shared memory primitives. On a Silicon Graphics system, for example, the file sgi.C implementing these classes is only about 240 lines. Silicon Graphics allows the launching of processes in the same address space using the sproc system call, and standard C++ memory allocators work without modification if an application is linked using the standard library for multiprocessor applications. Other architectures may require more work on shared memory allocation, but most of the other features should be easy to implement using standard system calls.

Care has been taken to restrict machine-specific code in OOSH to this specific layer.

4.5 Kernel Classes

The kernel classes are the layer of abstraction isolating machine-dependent classes from the rest of the code. Kernel classes are mostly used as building blocks for other classes.

The top of the class hierarchy is the class Object, which is an abstract class used to define common behaviour for most other classes including error handling and low-level allocators. There are two other classes used respectively for constructing free lists and allocating memory a page at a time: Free_objects and Free_page. Allocation of memory a page at a time is implemented to support potential future work on program structuring for efficient TLB usage (see 8.2.1).

Queues are implemented on top of class Queue (the head of the queue and iterators over elements); objects that can be queued are derived from Queued_object.

Class Synch_data presents an application-level interface to Synch_info (the machine-dependent class, which contains state identifying a specific barrier). Process is the application-level view of the class Machine_process, while Lock_data is the application-level view of Lock_info.

Locks and barriers are implemented by conceptually similar mechanisms. A lock or barrier is identified by a specific object that maintains its state (class Lock_data or Synch_data, respectively). A lock is held for the lifetime of a variable of class Lock, which is given a pointer to a specific Lock_data object, for example:

```
{ Lock error_region (output_lock);
    cerr << error_message << flush;
}
```

The same lock can be used somewhere else:

```
{ Lock debug_region (output_lock);
    cerr << debug_message << flush;
}
```

When the close of scope of a variable of class Lock is reached, the destructor is called. The constructor for Lock acquires the lock identified by the Lock_data pointer sent to it as an argument and saves a copy of the pointer in the new object of class Lock. The destructor for Lock releases the lock. Note that in each case, a local variable is being defined, and has to be given a name (error_region and debug_region in the two lock examples). Although the local name is not used anywhere else, such a variable does have to be given a name. Otherwise, the compiler is free to treat it as a temporary, and call the destructor immediately, instead of waiting for the name to go out of scope [Ellis and Stroustrup 1990, p 268].

The OOSH lock construct has the advantage that it is relatively easy to use, and it is not possible to forget to release a lock. For example, code in the SPLASH version of Barnes-Hut uses complicated logic with a flag to determine which code should be executed in the loop which inserts a body into the octree, as well as whether to terminate the loop. The OOSH version of the code uses a return statement at the point the body has been inserted, and relies on the C++ compiler to release the lock by calling the destructor.

(a) column:

```
if (*insert_pos==NULL)
{ Lock insert_lock(lock_data);
//still NULL?
    if (*insert_pos==NULL)
    { *insert_pos = this;
        return; // (1)
    }
// (2)
}
if ( xxxx ) { …
```

(b) column:

```
if(*insert_pos==NULL)
{  LOCK(CellLock);
   /* still NULL? */
    if (*insert_pos==NULL)
    { *insert_pos = p;
        flag=FALSE;
    }
    UNLOCK(CellLock);
}
if (flag && ( xxxx )) { …
```

(a) OOSH approach   **(b) SPLASH approach**

Figure 4.2 OOSH *vs.* SPLASH Locks

from Barnes-Hut; detail left out—the OOSH version relies on the compiler to release the lock in the Lock object destructor at (1) or (2); on the other hand, in the SPLASH code, the programmer must contrive code to be sure the lock is unlocked exactly once and under the right conditions

As an example, the two approaches are given in figure 4.2, which contains code from Barnes-Hut, with detail left out, to illustrate the principle. In 4.2a, the OOSH version, the lock is released either when the destructor is called at the return (labelled "(1)") —or at the exit of scope of the Lock variable (at the comment labelled "(2)"). In 4.2b, the SPLASH version, explicit LOCK and UNLOCK macros are used, and the logic to ensure that UNLOCK is correctly used is comparatively complicated.

To avoid having the untidy situation of more than one UNLOCK macro for a single LOCK, the SPLASH implementers chose to set a flag inside the inner if statement. The flag can then be tested at later points in the loop to ensure that no further execution occurs. If the SPLASH coders had instead chosen to use a return statement at the point where no further work is required, they would have had to remember to put an UNLOCK in two places, which requires careful reading by the programmer to be sure that the construct is correct.

Barriers are implemented roughly the same way as locks. A barrier has no concept of opening and closing, but to allow for the possibility of absorbing minor load imbalances between phases of a timestep, barriers are implemented in OOSH with two phases: announcing arrival at the barrier, and waiting for all other processes to announce their arrival at the barrier. These two phases are also implemented using constructors and destructors. In principle it is possible to put code which is not dependent on synchronization between these two parts of the barrier. Usage of a barrier looks like this:

```
{   Delayed_synch wait_name (delay_name);
    // can insert code not dependent on synchronizing here
}
```

where delay_name is a pointer to a Synch_data object, and wait_name is a local name. As with locks, the local name is essential to prevent the destructor from being called prematurely, but can also be useful for identifying this synchronization point to the human reader of the code.

If no code is inserted inside the scope of a Delayed_synch,, the effect is the same as a conventional barrier.

One other group of classes of general use is Array1D, Array2D and Array3D, which respectively implement arrays of 1, 2 and 3 dimensions. These array classes can store pointers to any descendant of class Object and their size can be dynamically determined when they are constructed. Their major advantage over conventional arrays is dynamic size determination. In principle, the same effect can be achieved in C by implementing multi-dimensional arrays as arrays of pointers [Kernighan and Richie 1978]. Classes which redefine the array indexing operator allow redefined indexing to be done more transparently.

4.6 Higher-Level Classes

The remaining three layers of OOSH are space, environment and command. These classes are more likely to be specialized by inheritance for a specific the application than the kernel classes.

Only the space classes—which implement a hierarchical division of space into units of work—are described in detail, as the other classes are incidental to understanding the architecture of OOSH. The class described in some detail here are:

- `Precinct`—the smallest unit that can be scheduled or used in load balancing; if object-blocking is possible, the precinct is the unit to be blocked: the major function implemented in a precinct is asking space units to work

- `Space_unit`—an atomic unit of work in terms of application semantics: a specific application must at least implement the `do_work` function for a space unit

- `Proc_data`—data specific to a process, including a queue of precincts: the major function which must be implemented for this class is `get_load`, to do load allocation

Division into precincts and space units is convenient because in some applications, it may be natural to break the problem down into smaller units of work than would not be too small to schedule efficiently. Such smaller units of work would then be space units, and they would be grouped together to form precincts.

A precinct is an important part of an OOSH application. Its size should be chosen carefully, in terms of the amount of work it represents. To block the algorithm for a specific cache size, a precinct should not reference more data than will fit in the cache. At the same time, to avoid making process dispatch overhead too large, a precinct should not be smaller than it needs to be. Choosing an appropriate size for a precinct is highly dependent on characteristics of a specific application and machine.

Precincts define one more level of predefined control: each precinct has a member function `try_to_work` which is invoked from `Process::dispatch`. Unlike `dispatch`, however, `try_to_work` can be completely replaced in an application (recall from the discussion in section 4.3 that new classes should not be derived from `Process`). Pseudocode for `try_to_work` is given in figure 4.3.

Data private to a processor is stored in an object of a class derived from `Proc_data`. In section 4.3, the difference between the purpose of `Proc_data` an class `Process` is explained.

Class `Proc_data` in its predefined form includes the list of precincts owned by a processor, and member function `get_load` to do load allocation. Using `Proc_data` to do load allocation is natural because precincts and space units will not necessarily belong to the same processor after load is reallocated. It therefore does not make sense to use a precinct or a space unit of them as a container for load for a specific processor.

```
boolean Precinct::try_to_work (Proc_data *processor_data)
{    Space_unit *current;
     boolean work_done = false;
     while (can_work ( )) // app must define can_work ( )
     {    work_done = true;
          for (∀ unit ∈ space_units)
             unit->do_work (processor_data);
          step_final ( );
     }
     return work_done;
}
```

Figure 4.3 Default Per-Precinct Work

Environment classes initialize space and the kernel classes, and interpret command line arguments.

Command classes are optional: they are used to implement a simple command interpreter for applications that are interactively driven.

4.7 Application Implementation Issues

To implement a completely new application, one way of starting would be to do a trivial application in which no derived classes are defined, and build from there by defining classes specific to the application.

A minimal main program is illustrated in figure 4.4. This is a complete program (when linked to OOSH) that launches the number of processes given in the command line and terminates each after discovering that there are no precincts in the processor's queue.

To turn OOSH classes into a full application, classes would have to be defined for application-specific precincts, space units, simulation environment and per-processor data—and any other classes relevant to the application.

```
#include "Space.h"
#include "Environment.h"
#include "Command.h"
#include "Kernel.inl"

void main (int argc, char *argv[ ])
{  Simulation_environment min_env (argc, argv, "");
   Command::init_commands ( );
   const int num_procs = Environment_object::get_num_procs ( );
   Process ** processes = new Process* [num_procs];
   Proc_data ** proc_data = new Proc_data* [num_procs];
   for (int i = 0; i < num_procs; i++)
      proc_data[i] = new Proc_data (num_procs, i);
   for (i = 1; i < num_procs; i++)
      processes[i] = new Process (i, &min_env, proc_data[i]);
   // proc 0 runs on this processor - launch last
   processes[0] = new Process (0, &min_env, proc_data[0]);
   for (i = 0; i < num_procs; i++)
      delete processes[i];
}
```

Figure 4.4 Minimal Application

The steps required for porting an existing application to OOSH depend on how closely the application structure corresponds to the library's flow of control. One approach is to start with the real-world problem being solved, and identify objects using an object-oriented design methodology [Booch 1991]. This would work to the extent that the goal of spatial decomposition was observed; otherwise fitting the resulting design to OOSH could be difficult. Rather than a classic object-oriented design strategy, it might be better to start with attempting to identify space units and precincts in the real-world problem. A possible view of the benefit of starting with OOSH rather than programming from scratch is that OOSH provides a start towards an object-oriented design.

A key factor, once the major objects have been identified, is identifying shared and non-shared data, and ensuring that data is grouped into padded and aligned objects to avoid false sharing. Working towards fitting real-world objects to OOSH classes would be a helpful strategy, since this strategy would be a short cut to both producing an object-oriented design and matching the design to OOSH. Another important aspect of the design is attempting to decompose the real-world space in such a way that interactions are local as far as possible, which would fit the OOSH emphasis on spatial decomposition with minimal communication. Again, relating real-world objects to OOSH classes as soon as possible would probably facilitate the process described here.

Identification of the spatial decomposition should also lead to defining the outer level control flow of the code. Once a decision has been made as to how the application's outer level of control maps on to the OOSH library, earlier decisions as to which objects are best represented as precincts, space units etc. can be validated — and possibly altered.

If a spatial decomposition can be found, units of work can be grouped into precincts, the size of which should be kept flexible, to allow for blocking to different cache sizes. Even if spatial decomposition cannot be carried as far as identifying units of work with purely local interactions, precincts can still be used as the unit of dispatching work, and should be defined in any implementation.

As part of the process of identifying precincts, any opportunities for blocking should be sought. If blocking avoids the alternative of many references to data across widely spaced points in a time step, it is likely to result in a major improvement.

If the code is being ported to OOSH from existing shared-memory multiprocessor code, attention also has to be paid to whether it relies on fork semantics. If it does, global variables that are assumed to be copied to each process have to be moved to the per-process data (derived from OOSH class `Proc_data`).

Once all these decisions have been taken, the final step before coding is to decide on the trade-off between maximizing the benefit of using OOSH, versus minimal change to the original code. The trade-off can be quantified with the aid of profiling tools such as are typically found on UNIX systems—or performance visualization tools such as Chiron [Goosen *et al.* 1993]—which can give an indication as to the potential for improvement of the original code.

In some cases, if an existing well-optimized application is being ported to OOSH, major restructuring will not be worth the effort. In others, where the original application has poor cache behaviour, a major restructuring will be worthwhile. When an application is being coded from scratch, this trade-off does not apply. In some cases a spatial decomposition may be easy to achieve. In other cases, it may not be worth the effort to find a spatial decomposition, because the amount of computation in relation to cache misses is high enough for cache misses to be insignificant. The definition of a "high" amount of communication relative to cache misses depends on the characteristics of available machines: as the memory-processor speed gap widens, applications previously considered high in computation in relation to misses may become candidates for implementation using OOSH.

Chapter 5, which explains the choice of applications used to measure performance, takes points raised in this section into account.

Commentary

Some of the detail here is not of great interest for general-purpose applications but there are ideas that are generally useful. The concept of using a constructor and a destructor to encapsulate opening and closing code for example is generally applicable (and can also for example be used to open and close a graphics context).

Retrofitting a class library to existing code is always messier than doing an object-oriented design from scratch. For this reason, some of the design trade-offs made here may not always apply. However, application restructuring to improve multiprocessor performance will not always start from a non-object-oriented base.

5. Choice Of Applications

5.1 Introduction

This chapter explains the reasons for selecting each application, including both issues most relevant to the goals of the research, and more general reasons for choosing applications to measure.

The OOSH library is primarily designed to facilitate spatial decomposition as a strategy for reducing cache misses. It is therefore important that it be used to implement at least one program which naturally fits this model. At the same time, it is useful to investigate generality of OOSH by implementing at least one program which does not fit the model as well. In this way it is possible to quantify the benefits of OOSH both on a program to which it is well suited, as well as on one which may take extra work to convert to a spatial decomposition.

A starting point of this research is that it should be applicable to real-world problems potentially of interest to either large numbers of people, or to those spending large sums of money on expensive solutions such as traditional supercomputers. Each application implemented has to exactly fit these criteria, as long as it is similar to others that do and can be used as an archetype for such problems. The choice of applications is also influenced by the need to produce results comparable with other research.

Simulations of large-scale real-world phenomena are generally challenging problems that require large amounts of computation, so this is a useful class of application to support both because many such problems are widely useful and because they usually require expensive supercomputers to solve effectively.

The broad class of simulations can further be broken down into discrete event simulations and timestepped simulations. Given the major differences in flow of control between these two styles of simulation, it is not realistic to attempt to build a relatively simple library such as OOSH that will support both.

The widely used Stanford SPLASH benchmarks for shared-memory multi-processors [Singh *et al.* 1992b][*] include a number of timestepped simulations. Consequently, timestepped simulations are an obvious choice in order to obtain results comparable to other published work.

This chapter goes on to establish more specific criteria for choosing applications, in section 5.2. These criteria are based on the need to test the generality of the research, as well as to exercise OOSH on a range of different styles of application.

Reasons for selecting each of three application are presented by relating the applications to the criteria, in sections 5.3 to 5.5. Where relevant, history of each application is presented to add depth to justifying its selection. Presentation of more detail of each application is deferred to Chapter 6, where implementation is described.

---

[*] The Barnes-Hut application is not in the published SPLASH report: it is however documented in the latest version of the report at the ftp site www.flash.stanford.edu.

The chapter concludes with a summary in section 5.6 of the characteristics of each application, and relates them to the selection criteria.

5.2 Criteria

The OOSH library is mainly designed for time-stepped simulations in which a spatial decomposition can be found. However some generality is desirable, given the potential for reuse of object-oriented code.

Consequently, measurement of some diversity of style of application is desirable. On the other hand, some limit has to be placed on the style of application that is supported. In general, the OOSH framework does not specifically require that a program constructed on it be a time-stepped simulation, or that it be decomposed spatially. However, any application that does not fit the description of a spatially decomposed time-stepped simulation does not use all the features provided by the library.

The following criteria are used in selecting applications, with the aim of covering a range of variations from most likely to benefit from OOSH to least likely:

1. *locality of data accesses*—at least one application should mainly reference a small part of the overall data set in a specific part of the computation, and another should use a large part of the data set to recompute local state; good locality fits the spatial decomposition strategy of this research well—especially the potential to exploit object blocking—whereas the other case does not

2. *style of synchronization*—global versus local—at least one program is included that only requires synchronization between nearest neighbours (except at start,

finish and load balance time), and at least one which requires global synchronization per time step; the first case fits the OOSH model of distributed synchronization well; the latter is more suited to barriers

3. *complexity of data structures and algorithms*—at least one application should have data which is natural to implement as objects, possibly with complex algorithms including recursion; another should be more natural to program using arrays and algorithms which could be programmed easily in a language like FORTRAN, to cover a good fit and a poor fit to the object-oriented strategy of OOSH

Time-stepped simulations covering these criteria are to be found in the SPLASH benchmarks. In addition to taking the above criteria into account, the three applications are intended to cover the following variations:

- one that is a good fit to OOSH, but which has poor performance in the SPLASH version (MP3D)

- one that is a well optimized application from SPLASH but is harder to fit to OOSH (Barnes-Hut)

- one that is representative of dusty decks or legacy code, in that it is relatively straightforward FORTRAN-style array code, which is a poor fit to OOSH (Water)

The following three sections describe each of the three applications used in measurement, in turn.

5.3 MP3D

MP3D is a particle-based simulation of a wind tunnel. It is chosen to illustrate both spatial decomposition and local synchronization. It is a relatively simple program in terms of algorithms and data structures, but does have obvious candidates for implementation as objects (particles and cells, for example).

MP3D only requires local communication. Space is divided into unit cubes called *cells*, and particles move through space with velocity such that they never move more than one cell length in a timestep. Consequently, cells need only communicate with nearest neighbours to decide if they can move to the next timestep.

It is possible to do all processing of each particle to update its state for a new timestep before communication is necessary. It is therefore possible to block the application, so that all processing for a given timestep for a given cell is done at once. A cell is a small unit of work to schedule at once, so cells are grouped into precincts. The actual size of a precinct is determined by the cache size of a specific machine on which MP3D is run, and the likely number of particles per cell for a specific wind tunnel example. If the precinct size is made larger, scheduling overhead lower is reduced, but if it is made too large, the effect of blocking is lost. A smaller precinct size also makes it easier to allocate load accurately, so choice of precinct size is non-trivial.

Since a particle is only referenced at two phases of a time step (moving and collision), blocking should not be a major win. However, it is worth implementing as part of this research, to measure how big an effect it is.

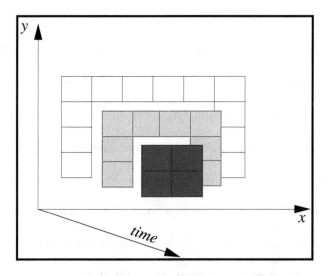

Figure 5.1 Effect of Local Synchronization

parts of space can advance a step ahead of nearest neighbours
(darker shading is used to show space further advanced in times)

In addition, since only local communication is needed, minor load imbalances can be absorbed by allowing a region of space to advance as long as it does not do more than one step while waiting for its neighbours. This is an example of the value of distributed synchronization, and is illustrated in figure 5.1.

A precinct can be left a step behind all of its neighbours, which then have to wait until it catches up. The tardy precinct can be processed twice to catch up, further exploiting blocking.

Since many details of MP3D have been improved, it is useful to compare MP3D against 2 earlier versions with different degrees of optimization for a cache-based architecture.

MP3D has been the subject of a restructuring study that provided the starting point for this research [Cheriton *et al.* 1991b], and has also been modified by others who have used it as a benchmark [Hagersten *et al.* 1992]. The earliest version of MP3D used in this research is poorly structured because it was derived from code for a vector machine [McDonald and Baganoff 1988]. More detail of problems with the original MP3D is presented in section 6.2.1.

5.4 Barnes-Hut

Barnes-Hut has both complex data structures and algorithms. It requires global synchronization several times each timestep. It is a good candidate for an object-oriented implementation, but its synchronization and communication pattern is not a good fit to OOSH. However, the fact that it uses fewer features of OOSH than MP3D makes it useful as a basis for evaluating specific features of the library (i.e., there are fewer variables in comparing the OOSH version with the original SPLASH version).

The original C code relies heavily on type casts and checking of flags to implement and differentiate between similar data structures—a style of code that translates naturally to object-oriented code. A different derived class is used for the each variant; dynamic dispatch using virtual functions (method invocation) replaces checking flags.

Although the SPLASH code has parts that are object-oriented in style, the code as a whole is not particularly cleanly structured, and makes extensive use of global variables. Some non-obvious code is a result of optimizations. For example, when a body's position in space is recomputed (once per time step), the new result is computed in a global variable to avoid cache invalidations as other processors use other parts of the body's data to compute the position of other bodies. It would be easy to tidy the code up in the SPLASH version, as was done in the OOSH version. Something that would be more difficult to tidy up in the SPLASH version is the extensive use of type casts of pointers, based on the value of a flag. This kind of code is much more readable in an object-oriented form, where the C++ virtual function mechanism is used to execute the correct code depending on the type of object a pointer currently points to.

The major data structure is an *octree* (a tree with up to 8 descendants at each interior node). Interior nodes represent regions in space, and leaves represent bodies. An *n*–body gravitation computation requires computation of gravitation between all pairs of bodies. However the Barnes-Hut algorithm reduces computation by treating groups of bodies further than some cut-off distance from a given body as a single point mass. The algorithm improves the complexity from the more obvious $O(n^2)$ to $O(n\log n)$ per timestep [Barnes and Hut 1986]. Interior nodes of the tree are similar to bodies, when they are used as point masses in the approximation. It is the similarity between bodies and interior nodes that is an obvious candidate for inheritance (i.e., derived classes from a common base class).

Figure 5.2 illustrates how bodies in 2-dimensional space can be represented using a *quadtree*. An octree is similar, though it requires eight branches in an interior node to represent 3-dimensional space in the same way. Each interior node (called a *cell*) divides space in half in each dimension, and also contains centre of mass data representing all bodies below it in the tree. Bodies are represented as leaves of the tree.

Gravity computation is done using a recursive tree traversal.

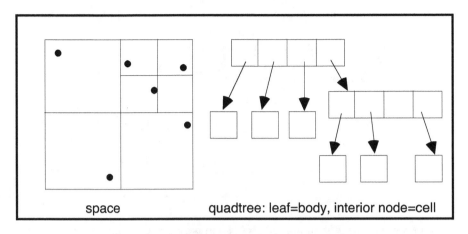

| space | quadtree: leaf=body, interior node=cell |

Figure 5.2 Quadtree Representation of Space

3-dimensional space is presented in the same way using an octree

The SPLASH code includes a relatively complex optional load balancing strategy, *orthogonal regional bisection* (ORB). ORB divides space into regions of equal cost recursively, using another tree. Cost is measured by counting the number of interactions for each body.

However, the ORB strategy does not give an appreciable advantage over dividing space using the simpler strategy of dividing the octree into equal *costzones*. A costzone is a group of bodies contiguous in the leaves of the tree, which have a processor's share of the overall cost. The drawback of the costzones strategy is that it is possible that adjacent leaves in a tree are not adjacent in space, leading to a processor not processing bodies as close as possible in space. While ORB overcomes this problem, it introduces extra overhead which cancels out the gain [Singh *et al.* 1992a].

Since it does not appear to be worth the effort required to implement it, the ORB strategy is not used in the OOSH version. Implementation would be fairly straightforward, based on the SPLASH code.

5.5 Water

Water is simple algorithmically and does not have complex data structures. It also requires repeated global synchronization between phases of each timestep. The original program was written in FORTRAN and ported to C. Although some changes to data structures have been made, the code is still rather FORTRAN-like. For example, short variable names are used, and most separately compiled files contain a single large function corresponding to a FORTRAN subroutine.

The program computes forces and potentials inside a system of water molecules. The computation is done over timesteps until steady state. Each time step requires setting up and solving Newtonian equations of motion. One phase of the timestep loop, computing inter-molecular forces, is $O(n^2)$ and dominates execution time as the other phases are $O(n)$. The computation on a specific molecule requires information from half of the other molecules in the simulation [Singh *et al.* 1992b].

Since the other two programs cover the other selection criteria adequately, the OOSH version of Water does not exercise the library significantly, and is used as an example of how minimal use of the object-oriented features may be used to quickly port code to OOSH. It is also used as a basis for a rough estimate of the overhead of using the library without any attempt at optimization or use of its performance enhancement features, not even padding and aligning to cache blocks.

5.6 Summary

Although three applications cannot be expected to cover the entire field of variations on styles of application, the chosen applications fit the criteria for selection.

MP3D has potential for spatial decomposition, whereas Barnes-Hut does not have an obvious spatial decomposition. Water has some spatial locality, but less than MP3D. MP3D only requires local synchronization, whereas the other two applications require global synchronization.

Both MP3D and Water have fairly simple data structures which, in the original implementations, were implemented as arrays of floating point numbers. MP3D is used to illustrate the potential of OOSH for reimplementation using spatial decomposition, distributed synchronization and padded and aligned objects. Water is used to illustrate the overhead of OOSH on code in which no improvements have been made. Barnes-Hut on the other hand has complex data structures, which are easier to understand when implemented using classes and inheritance than in their original C form.

MP3D and Water both have relatively simple control logic. Barnes-Hut, on the other hand, has recursive tree traversals for gravitation computation and load allocation.

These three applications therefore exercise the library over a range of variations on complexity of implementation. They also provide data points for the value of the library according to how well the style of a specific application fits its programming model. While other applications may have significantly different characteristics, the chosen applications illustrate that OOSH is reasonably general in its applicability.

6. Application Implementations

6.1 Introduction

The three applications involve significantly different OOSH implementation strategies, reflecting the goal of evaluating the generality of OOSH—and the fact that they represent different degrees of fit to the OOSH programming model.

MP3D is substantially rewritten from the original shared-memory code, Barnes-Hut is a complete rewrite but with essentially the same order of execution as the SPLASH version, and Water is changed as little as possible. The MP3D rewrite reflects the fact that earlier versions of MP3D had poor spatial decomposition, which is reflected in their poor cache behaviour (as can be seen in Chapter 7). Barnes-Hut on the other hand has reasonably good cache behaviour in its SPLASH implementation, and is therefore a less clear target for a complete rewrite.

This chapter presents the strategies for implementation of each application in turn, in sections 6.2 to 6.4. For each application, its original structure and structure in its final form as implemented for OOSH are presented, followed by an estimate of the amount of work required for each approach to implementation. These estimates are intended to guide others considering using OOSH.

After each application is described, the chapter concludes with section 6.5, containing a summary of findings on experience with implementation of applications using OOSH.

6.2 MP3D

MP3D is a particle-based wind tunnel simulation. A rectangular box represents the wind tunnel, with some geometry of interest placed in it. Space is divided into unit cubes called *cells*. A cell is used as the smallest unit of space for measurement of simulation properties, and for detecting particle-particle collisions.

Each timestep of the simulation proceeds through the following phases:

1. move — move particles according to their velocity

2. boundary — adjust velocity of bodies that have hit the walls or the object in the wind tunnel according to boundary conditions and move particle back into free space

3. collide — decide if a collision occurs for each randomly selected pair in each cell and adjust velocity, conserving momentum

A full search of potential collision partners would be $O(n^2)$ per time step. Instead, randomly pairing particles within a cell and using a decision function to decide whether they should collide makes each time step $O(n)$ [McDonald and Baganoff 1988].

6.2.1 Original Structure

MP3D in its original form (labelled in earlier work as MP3D–0 [Cheriton *at al.* 1991b, 1993]) is a classic central work pool style shared memory parallel program, without much change in data structures from the original Cray implementation.

Each timestep, the following steps are performed:

1. move particles

2. boundary collisions: move particles back into free space

3. do collisions with other particles based on decision function within cells

4. add new particles to replace those that left the wind tunnel and to maintain flow

5. update the reservoir (used to generate random numbers for collisions and generating new particles)

Different phases are separated by barriers.

Each attribute of a particle is represented in a separate array (for example, the particles' x co-ordinates are stored in an array called x; the y co-ordinates in an array called y, etc.). This organization causes a high degree of false sharing. In addition, the particles have no processor affinity: each processor contends for the next index into the particle arrays, with a high probability that a given particle will not be processed by the same processor twice in succession, even within different phases of a single timestep.

Collision pairing is done by checking a pointer in an array of cells. If the pointer is null, the particle is inserted into the cell. If the pointer is not null, the particle found through the pointer is a candidate for collision and the collision decision rule is used to decide if it should be collided. After this step, the cell's particle pointer is reset to null. The strategy is designed to randomize the selection of collision partners.

MP3D–0, as a result of its particle data structures and collision handling, has poor cache behaviour, which is also reflected in poor performance on a real machine

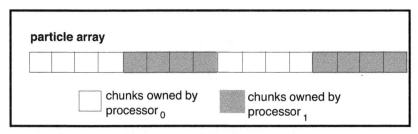

Figure 6.1 MP3D–SPLASH Particle Organization
illustrated here for 2 processors

(see section 7.3.2). Simulations of the ParaDiGM architecture show that it has a miss ratio of 30% (of references to shared data) or more, depending on cache block size. The figure increases steadily as the block size increases: for a 128-byte block, the ratio is 46% [Cheriton *at al.* 1991b]. Some detail of work on restructuring MP3D which formed the basis of this work is presented in Appendix A.

The SPLASH version of MP3D replaces the particle arrays by an single array of C structs, which is partitioned into *chunks*, each of which is intended to be an integral number of cache blocks in size.

Each processor moves chunks, as is illustrated in figure 6.1. However, collision pairing is still done using an array of cells. The new organization reduces cache misses in the move phase, but does nothing to reduce misses for the collision phase. Another improvement on MP3D–0 is that each processor can identify its chunks of particles using a local counter, eliminating the need for contending for a shared counter in the move phase.

The SPLASH implementation is not blocked: the order in which particles are processed depends on where they fall in the particle arrays, which is unrelated to locality in the simulation space. Consequently, the gain in locality in chunking the arrays does not result in any improvement in locality in selection of collision partners and in updating cell data, which is done every time a particle is moved.

6.2.2 OOSH Implementation

The OOSH implementation is designed to maximize processor affinity, while using the library's padded and aligned allocators to eliminate false sharing.

Processor affinity is achieved at the expense of both more complex load balancing, and explicit randomization of collision partners.

Space is divided into *precincts*, rectangular regions of fixed size. Each precinct is the minimum unit of work allocation, rather than a particle (as in MP3D–0).

Taking advantage of the need to synchronize with space no more than one cell away from a given cell, *distributed synchronization* is used. Distributed synchronization relies on comparing local clocks in adjacent precincts to see if a given precinct can move, rather than using a global barrier. In some circumstances, it is possible for a precinct to move 2 timesteps at a time, if precinct p did not move at timestep i, but all its neighbours did. Its neighbours now cannot move until precinct p has moved. However, since they are all now one timestep ahead, p can move for 2 steps. Distributed synchronization has two major advantages:

- short-term load imbalance, such as may occur between phases of a timestep, can be absorbed

- memory accesses to determine whether a processor may proceed are distributed over a number of different data structures (the neighbour holding up each precinct which may not proceed), which removes the problem of a hot spots

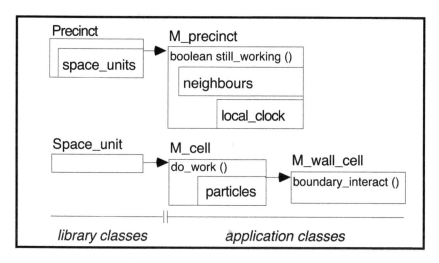

Figure 6.2 Derivation of Major MP3D Classes from OOSH
showing major new function and data members

associated with spinning on a global synchronization variable [Mellor-Crumney and Scott 1991]

Figure 5.1 in Section 5.3 illustrates how distributed synchronization can allow part of the simulation to be ahead of other parts.

MP3D precincts are implemented as OOSH precincts with the addition of neighbour lists for distributed synchronization. Each precinct has a queue of space units, and each space unit has a queue of particles, which are implemented on top of queued objects.

Cells are implemented as space units, with boundary cells derived from cells to implement different behaviour for boundary conditions.

Figure 6.2 illustrates the relationship between MP3D classes and OOSH classes.

In addition to those illustrated, the Array3D class is used to look up precincts and cells. Given floating-point particle co-ordinates, the cell in which the particle belongs is found by truncating the co-ordinates and using the resulting integers as indices into the cell array. Similarly, precincts are looked up using a precinct array, with indices scaled from the range of cell indices to the range of precinct indices.

Each precinct's work consists of checking if its neighbours have all advanced enough for it to continue. If they have the precinct processes each of its cells. Each cell in turn moves and collides its particles. A given precinct processes its cells as many times as possible. If it has dropped a step behind, it can process its cells twice, as described earlier in this section.

MP3D is relatively slow to change its pattern of work (particles on average stay in the same cell for three time steps), so load balancing is not done every timestep in the call to get_load. Instead, it is only done once at the start of each run. Unlike the other examples, MP3D has a simple command interpreter, with commands such as advance *n* steps, print a report, and quit. Consequently, a long run can easily be divided into stages, before each of which load is reallocated. Other work on MP3D suggests that doing a load balance every 100 steps may be sufficient [McDonald 1991].

The per-precinct part of the dispatch loop, try_to_work, is used, but step_final is not. Work on each cell is dispatched if an M_precinct's can_work function returns true. To determine if a precinct can work, can_work checks if the precinct's local_clock is before the global stop time, and that none of the precinct's nearest neighbours is behind. If all these conditions are met, all the precinct's cells do their work for the timestep.

A complication resulting from the processor affinity of MP3D–OOSH is that particle collision partner selection has to be explicitly randomized. MP3D–0 relies on random allocation of particles to processors; with particles in a queue which is accessed by one processor, implicit randomization no longer occurs. Explicit randomization adds significant overhead: before collisions are performed the particle queue is ordered using a table of random numbers.

6.2.3 Amount of Work

It is difficult to accurately quantify the effort needed to convert MP3D to OOSH since it was the first application worked on and effort required to design the library is hard to factor out. Given the library and the same access to the original implementer, a similar application could probably be rewritten in about 6 months of intensive effort.

Access to the original implementer was essential for two reasons:

1. the code is nondeterministic—the order of particle collision is random and depends on a deliberate race condition—so help was needed in testing output (testing could not be done by a simple comparison of numbers from the previous version)

2. parts of the code were obscure; it wasn't clear if non-obvious features were bugs (some bugs were in fact found)

The time put into MP3D was approximately 2 years, but much of that time was spent on work that need not be repeated, such as exploring the possibility of using the optimistic model of simulation [Machanick 1992], and investigating how best to use C++.

6.3 Barnes-Hut

6.3.1 Original Structure

Each timestep of the original Barnes-Hut is divided into 6 major phases, with barriers to synchronize between the phases:

1. load bodies into tree (each cell uses a lock drawn from a pool stored in a lock array so this can be done in parallel)

2. find centre of mass moving up the tree

3. allocate load based on estimate of work done on each body last timestep

4. compute forces (most of execution time)

5. advance bodies' positions and velocities

6. compute global constants and do optional output

The major data structures of interest in the SPLASH version of Barnes-Hut are C structs node, body and cell. A node is conceptually an abstract type, used only for a pointer the type of which is resolved dynamically by looking up a type field. A node pointer can point to either a body (leaf) or a cell (interior node of tree).

Bodies and cells, though accessed mainly through pointers, are allocated in arrays to make load allocation and initialization between timesteps simpler.

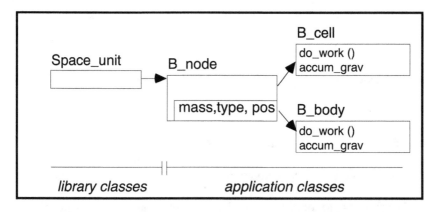

Figure 6.3 Derivation of Major Barnes-Hut classes from OOSH
showing major new function and data members

6.3.2 OOSH Implementation

In the OOSH implementation of Barnes-Hut, a node class is derived from the OOSH space unit class, and bodies and cells are both derived from cells. Where the SPLASH version uses a flag to differentiate node types during gravitation computation, the OOSH version uses dynamic dispatch of virtual functions which differ between cells and bodies.

Although a B_precinct class is defined, there is only one instance per processor, since a coarser grain of load allocation than a body is not needed in this application.

Since global synchronization is needed, barriers are retained.

The biggest conceptual change from the SPLASH implementation is implementing bodies and cells as separately allocated objects rather than as an array, to facilitate padding and aligning. Some of the initialization code, as well as load allocation, is slightly more complex than the SPLASH version.

The major classes are illustrated in figure 6.3.

The `dispatch` loop is fully used in Barnes-Hut. The call to `get_load` divides load up according to the costzones strategy (see section 5.4), the processor's precinct asks all its bodies to do their gravitation computation through the `try_to_work` call and `step_final` does the output and global counters computation stage of the timestep.

6.3.3 Amount of Work

It took approximately 6 months to rewrite Barnes-Hut, including a fair amount of time spent on performance debugging. The implementation time again is longer than it would be with a repeat exercise, as some time was spent in assisting with the design and implementation of the Chiron performance visualization system [Goosen et al. 1993].

Although Barnes-Hut is a more complex program than the others implemented for this research, the overall structure of the code of the SPLASH version is reasonably clear. There is however some obscure coding at the detailed level. Some examples include:

1. importing a `.c` file (the standard programmer's convention in C is that a `.c` file is compiled; a `#include` directive is only used for `.h` files — but this convention is not enforced by the compiler)

2. use of global variables for intermediate results to avoid writing to shared data in the gravity update phase

3. convoluted logic in the function to decide which branch of the tree to take for a given particle

4. extensive optional code for experimental load balancing strategies

However, unlike MP3D (see 6.2.3), the code is deterministic and therefore gives repeatable results. It is thus relatively straightforward to test new versions by comparing intermediate and final results across implementations.

6.4 Water

6.4.1 Original Structure

Each timestep, the program goes through the following phases:

1. calculate predicted values of variables

2. compute intra-molecular forces for atoms

3. computer inter-molecular forces—the only $O(n^2)$ phase

4. correct the predicted values from step 1, using values from steps 2 and 3

5. boundaries: put molecules back into the box

6. compute system kinetic energy

7. if an output step, calculate potential energy and print output

Although the program does not have the degree of locality of MP3D, each processor only communicates with half the molecules in the rest of the simulation. For a sufficiently large data set, this may be seen as global communication. In practice, since the algorithm is $O(n^2)$ per time step, data sets tend to be smaller than for MP3D or Barnes-Hut. Molecules are stored in an array which is partitioned between processors. In the one major change from the original FORTRAN version, each molecule's data is stored in a C `struct` for better locality and reduced false sharing [Singh *et al*. 1992b].

The outer level of control is fairly straightforward with simple loops, but detail is not entirely transparent, as a result of widespread use of short undescriptive variable names.

6.4.2 OOSH Implementation

The OOSH implementation replaces the SPLASH main program almost entirely, and adds functions that access global data members of class `W_processor_data` (to replace references to globals).

The biggest changes result from the fact that the SPLASH version of Water relies heavily on UNIX `fork` semantics (variables are not shared unless explicitly allocated as shared), whereas OOSH uses the `sproc` system call (everything is in shared memory, except data allocated on the stack after a process is launched).

Consequently, globals that are private to a process by default in the SPLASH version have to be made explicitly non-shared by moving them to a per-process object (of class `W_processor_data`, derived from `Proc_data`). On the other hand, some global data that is intended to be shared is moved from an explicitly allocated structure called gl to being declared as static members of W_processor_data. In effect a static class member is a global variable that has its name in the scope of the class. With sproc semantics, static class members are global to all processors.

The dispatch loop is mostly not used in this case: the get_load and step_final functions are empty, and Precinct::try_to_work is implemented as a once-only call to the main computation routine of the original code, MDMAIN.

6.4.3 Amount of Work

The changes made to the original code fall into two major categories: changes to header files and initialization to fit the object-oriented approach of OOSH, and detailed editing of individual files.

The original code consists of 1333 lines of source code in .U files (to be processed into .c files by the Parmacs macros), and 151 lines of .H files (to be preprocessed into header files).

In the first category, the header files are almost completely rewritten (total 165 lines—still not very big), and the main program file water.U (211 lines) is replaced by W_main.C, W_environment.C and W_space.C (total 411 lines).

The remaining files are edited for the new class-based globals and shared data, a total of 143 lines changed out of 1122 (not counting trivial changes such as indentation).

In summary, about 24% of the code including declarations (header files) is substantially rewritten and about 13% of the rest edited.

As with Barnes-Hut, testing can easily be done by comparing output (and intermediate results) across implementations.

It should be possible in principle to do such changes on similar examples in about a week of concentrated effort.

6.5 Summary

Reimplementing an existing application, if experience reported here is typical, on top of OOSH can take anywhere from a week to 6 months (assuming that the time spent on MP3D is atypical—since the 2 years spent on MP3D included designing the library and pursuing blind alleys), depending on how much restructuring is done.

Given the huge range of variations in application characteristics, such an estimate is obviously only a first estimate of possible effort needed. Of more interest is the question as to whether OOSH is significantly more difficult to use than other strategies. It took about a week to convert Water from Parmacs macros to OOSH, without major rewriting. Most of the effort was fairly straightforward and such difficulties as there were, were the consequence of the lack of clarity of the original code, rather than any complexities introduced by OOSH. Experience with Water suggests that a minimal use of OOSH without attempting to fully exercise its features is no more difficult than use of the Parmacs macros. Any attempt at restructuring is harder to evaluate. However, implementing padded and aligned allocators on top of reusable code is likely to save time over an ad hoc strategy.

Where application semantics are close the OOSH model, it should be relatively quick and easy to implement a new application using OOSH. In cases where OOSH aids in the programming task, the remaining issue in deciding to use OOSH is whether it results in acceptable—ideally improved—performance. The following chapters, in which performance is measured and analyzed, aim to elucidate the circumstances under which OOSH is useful.

Commentary

MP3D was the first application I worked on, and the one that was in the worst shape to start with. To some extent, that made it a soft target. As it was originally structured, it might as well have been written in FORTRAN, it had so little structuring of its data. A program in which related data was already grouped into objects would not as easily yield gains.

Nonetheless, as the next chapter shows, there are performance wins to be had in more challenging cases.

7. Performance Results

7.1 Introduction

This chapter contains results of performance measurement. Measurement is done using the Mint MIPS architecture simulator [Veenstra 1993]. Mint is used mainly for pragmatic reasons: it is freely available, relatively easy to use, has reasonable performance and interfaces with other available tools.

More detailed reasons for using Mint are presented in section 2.5.

To compare results against a real machine, runs are done on a Silicon Graphics 4D/380, which is a generation behind current designs, but is suitable as a basis for comparison with simulations.

Section 7.2 describes the methodology for measurement, including more detail of the usage of Mint. This is followed by the results, in section 7.3.

The following section (7.4) of this chapter is an analysis of the measured results. First, the section contains a brief discussion of how the results are interpreted. The remainder of section 7.4 is broken down into findings relating to the value of completely restructuring code with poor cache characteristics, the value of a more maintainable style of code and the cost of a minimal use of the library.

The rationale for the breakdown of discussing results in 7.4 is that it corresponds to different degrees of desirability of using OOSH. If an application has inherently poor characteristics and needs to be completely rewritten, using OOSH has significant advantages, as is demonstrated with MP3D. If the application is reasonably well structured but coding is untidy and unmaintainable, rewriting it in an object-oriented style can benefit maintainability without compromising performance, as is demonstrated by experience with Barnes-Hut. If no work is put into using features of OOSH, there is some cost compared with a non-object-oriented approach, as is shown using Water.

In conclusion, in section 7.5, overall findings are summarized.

7.2 Methodology

The major focus of this research is the impact of architecture trends on programming strategy. For this reason, measurements are taken with a simulator set up first to have characteristics typical of a high-performance design at around 1990, then with characteristics of a machine with double the memory cost in CPU cycles. According to previous trends, over a period of 6 years, the relative cost of a memory access should double [Boland and Dollas 1994]. In practice, the change in the cost of cache misses is not so simple: newer machines tend to have larger blocks and larger caches, both of which increase the cost of handling a cache miss. However, to keep the number of variables under control, only the miss cost is varied in measurements reported on here.

See Appendix D for a more detailed discussion of miss costs on two different systems spaced approximately six years apart.

The simulation is set up with a miss time of 50 cycles for the slower version. 50 clock cycles is a good approximation to miss cost of L2 caches of the early 1990s

[Goosen 1991]. The future version is set up with a miss cost of 100 CPU cycles. An infinite cache model is used so that only misses caused by invalidation are modeled. Measuring misses due to invalidations is a good approximation to measuring overhead of multiprocessor communication, as another study has shown that misses other than those caused by invalidations tend to be invariant across variations in numbers of processors [Eggers and Katz 1989]. The simulator counts *cold start* (or *compulsory*) misses and these are subtracted from the total. The block size is set at 128 bytes, which is found on some new designs [Galles and Williams 1994].

For measuring blocking effects, a finite cache simulation is required, as blocking mainly saves on replacements. Given the fact that communication causes extra misses, blocking should be expected to have a bigger impact on uniprocessor runs, but measurement is also presented for multiprocessor runs.

More detail of the architecture simulation is given in Appendix B.

To check the results, run times are measured on a Silicon Graphics 4D/380 with 8 MIPS R3000 processors, clocked at 33MHz and 256Mbytes of RAM. The 4D/380 was designed in the late 1980s. It has 2 levels of cache: a 64K first-level data cache and a 256K second-level cache (both direct-mapped). The L1 block size is 32 bytes, and an L2 block is 64 bytes. The L2 miss cost is 1μs, about 30 cycles. In practice, performance should be similar to that of the simulated machine, since the 4D/380 has a less aggressive bus design than the simulated design (see B.3).

With the exception of the MP3D runs that are run for more time steps on the real machine, the same data set is used for simulations and runs on the real machine. A longer run of MP3D is used on the real machine for consistency with earlier published results. More detail of application parameters is given in Appendix C.

Since derived measures such as speedup can be computed in different ways [Crowl 1994], the basis on which the calculation is done is presented, where derived measures are used. In most cases, absolute numbers are also presented (e.g., run time in seconds).

For each simulation run, the following data is summarized:

1. the fraction of read misses

2. the fraction of write misses

3. the fraction of misses overall

4. the fraction of writes causing invalidations

5. speedup with misses costing both 50 and 100 CPU cycles (other measures are not significantly affected by this variation in the simulation)

Since cold-start misses are not counted, miss measures of 1-processor runs are all zero (as is expected for infinite caches), and are not recorded.

Overall misses are the more useful characterization of application behaviour in terms of memory cost; however a breakdown of misses into read and write misses can give hints as to why misses occur. The fraction of writes causing invalidations is useful as a measure of the amount of communication (false or real sharing is not distinguished). Speedup is with an infinite cache model does not reflect the effect of blocking (for which finite cache measures are used in 7.3.3). Also, the total amount of cache to increases with the number of processors, reducing replacement misses—

an effect that is not modeled by a infinite cache simulation. However, infinite cache measures are good predictors of scalability, since they emphasize misses caused by communication.

Since only the OOSH version of MP3D is blocked, finite cache and corresponding real machine measurements of MP3D are presented separately (7.3.3). The major variable is block size (taken here as average size of a precinct—the size varies according to particle distribution in space). Measurement is presented relative to MP3D-SPLASH, the better of the two non-OOSH variants. Run times are measured for both a realistic 1-million particle example, and the 8000 particle example used in other measurement. The 1-million particle example is bigger than the L2 caches on the real machine, but too big to be practical to simulate. The 8000 particle example, on the other hand, is bigger than the L1 caches on the real machine, and so provides some opportunity to both measure impacts on run time of blocking to the L1 cache, and simulation measurements.

7.3 Results

Simulation results for each application are presented followed by measured run times on a real machine. After measurements applicable to all applications, a set of measurements is presented to establish the impact of blocking on MP3D. In each case, discussion of results is limited to pointing out interesting detail; full discussion of the significance of results is deferred to section 7.4. The most important finding is that Barnes-Hut's performance improves by 20% on a simulated machine with a miss cost of 100 cycles.

processors	measure	MP3D–0	OOSH	SPLASH
1	speedup miss 50	0.45	0.37	1.00
	speedup miss 100	0.45	0.37	1.00
4	read misses	27.81%	0.06%	2.68%
	write misses	2.09%	0.02%	0.08%
	overall misses	21.44%	0.05%	1.74%
	invalidations	67.82%	0.10%	4.77%
	speedup miss 50	0.36	1.33	2.33
	speedup miss 100	0.20	1.33	1.64
8	read misses	33.85%	0.09%	3.16%
	write misses	5.00%	0.03%	0.14%
	overall misses	26.68%	0.07%	2.07%
	invalidations	72.53%	0.14%	5.61%
	speedup miss 50	0.49	2.24	4.09
	speedup miss 100	0.25	2.17	2.66
16	read misses	37.09%	0.12%	3.49%
	write misses	6.82%	0.03%	0.29%
	overall misses	29.58%	0.10%	2.34%
	invalidations	74.79%	0.18%	6.09%
	speedup miss 50	0.46	4.05	5.29
	speedup miss 100	0.23	3.79	2.72
32	read misses	39.14%	0.14%	3.72%
	write misses	6.92%	0.04%	0.62%
	overall misses	31.13%	0.11%	2.60%
	invalidations	75.76%	0.21%	6.36%
	speedup miss 50	0.44	6.21	4.65
	speedup miss 100	0.22	5.45	2.39

Table 7.1 MP3D Simulation Results

invalidations as a fraction of writes; no cold start misses; infinite cache; speedup relative to fastest uniprocessor run

7.3.1 Simulations

Measurements are taken for the three versions of MP3D, with 8000 particles, over 50 timesteps, in a wind tunnel with 20 by 28 by 6 cells. This is a small example (real examples typically have 1-million or more particles), so results should be treated with caution. As well as finite cache simulations in section 7.3.3, a bigger example is used on the real machine, as another data point for measuring blocking in the OOSH version. However, the 8000-particle example is big enough to measure communication costs.

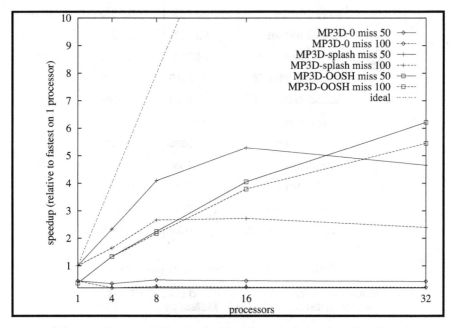

(a) speedups relative to fastest for each cache simulated

Figure 7.1 Simulator Measures for MP3D
continued on next page

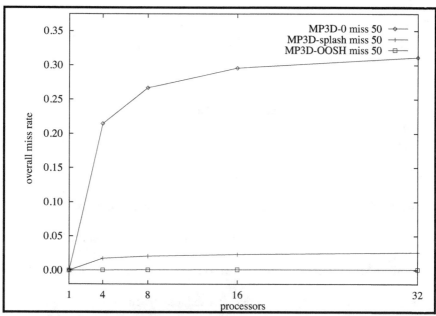

(b) misses (fraction of all references—except cold-start)

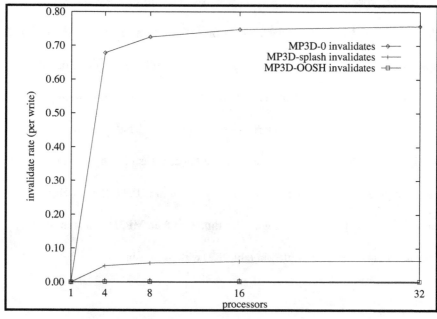

(c) invalidates (fraction of writes—except cold-start)

Figure 7.1 Simulator Measures for MP3D
continued from previous page

Results are presented in table 7.1, and graphed in figure 7.1. Miss rates are high, especially for the two poorly structured versions.

A high fraction of writes causes invalidations for MP3D-0 (over 75%) and the SPLASH version (over 6%—still high). Speedups are also relatively low (if the OOSH version achieves higher speedup with larger data—see 7.3.3).

Finally, the impact of a higher miss cost on each application is of interest. For example, on 32 processors, writes are 30 times more likely to result in invalidations for the SPLASH version than the OOSH version, and the miss ratio is 23.6 times higher. As a result, doubling the miss cost reduces speedup of the OOSH version (also on 32 processors) by only 12%, whereas speedup of the SPLASH version is reduced by 49%. In absolute terms, on 32 processors with miss cost 100, the OOSH version is 2.3 times faster (i.e., 130% faster) than the SPLASH version of MP3D.

Simulations of Barnes–Hut are run with 8K bodies, for 4 time steps—sufficient to capture communication characteristics of the program. There is limited blocking (a body has all gravitational effects computed at once, but is used again in other phases of the computation). Blocking is less important than in MP3D; Barnes-Hut does a lot more computation per body ($O(\log n)$) per time step than MP3D (constant time).

Barnes-Hut data is presented in table 7.2, with graphs in figure 7.2.

processors	measure	OOSH	SPLASH
1	speedup miss 50	1	0.93
	speedup miss 100	1	0.93
4	read misses	0.015%	0.049%
	write misses	0.00015%	0.016%
	overall misses	0.010%	0.037%
	invalidations	0.021%	0.063%
	speedup miss 50	3.87	3.58
	speedup miss 100	3.85	3.53
8	read misses	0.023%	0.073%
	write misses	0.00037%	0.021%
	overall misses	0.015%	0.053%
	invalidations	0.026%	0.073%
	speedup miss 50	7.38	6.82
	speedup miss 100	7.33	6.66
16	read misses	0.033%	0.096%
	write misses	0.0010%	0.026%
	overall misses	0.022%	0.070%
	invalidations	0.031%	0.075%
	speedup miss 50	14.5	13.3
	speedup miss 100	14.3	12.6
32	read misses	0.046%	0.12%
	write misses	0.0021%	0.029%
	overall misses	0.031%	0.084%
	invalidations	0.036%	0.077%
	speedup miss 50	27.9	24.5
	speedup miss 100	27.0	22.2

Table 7.2 Barnes-Hut Simulation Results

invalidations as a fraction of writes; no cold start misses; infinite cache

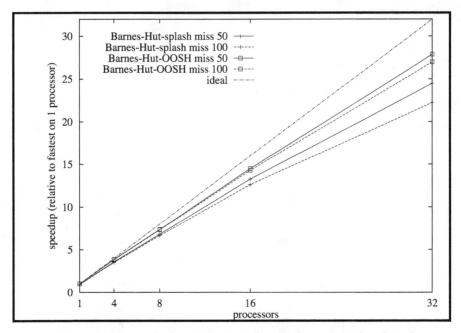

(a) speedups relative to fastest for each cache simulated

Figure 7.2 Simulator Measures for Barnes-Hut
continued on next page

Differences between the implementations are less sharp than with MP3D. However, the differences in misses between the OOSH and SPLASH versions are significant. There are also significantly more invalidations in the SPLASH version, reflecting false sharing. Speedups in all cases are much better than for MP3D. Even so, the SPLASH Barnes-Hut is impacted significantly more than the OOSH version by a slower simulated memory hierarchy.

Again using the comparison of speedups on 32-processor runs, OOSH Barnes-Hut's speedup is reduced by 3% when miss cost is doubled. By contrast, the SPLASH version's speedup is reduced by 9% when miss cost is doubled. With miss cost 100, OOSH Barnes-Hut is 22% faster than the SPLASH version.

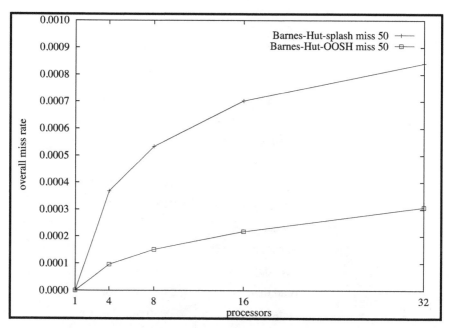

(b) misses (fraction of all references — except cold-start)

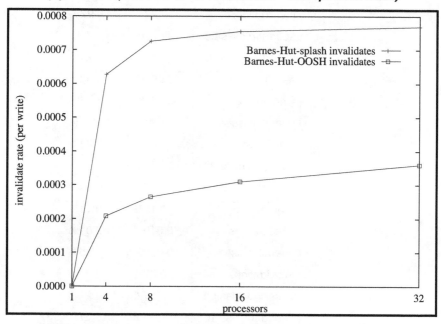

(c) invalidates (fraction of writes — except cold-start)

Figure 7.2 Simulator Measures for Barnes-Hut
continued from previous page

processors	measure	OOSH	SPLASH
1	speedup miss 50	0.98	1.00
	speedup miss 100	0.98	1.00
4	read misses	0.058%	0.056%
	write misses	0.00067%	0.00064%
	overall misses	0.043%	0.041%
	invalidations	0.17%	0.16%
	speedup miss 50	3.75	3.82
	speedup miss 100	3.70	3.77
8	read misses	0.082%	0.082%
	write misses	0.0020%	0.0019%
	overall misses	0.062%	0.062%
	invalidations	0.22%	0.22%
	speedup miss 50	7.40	7.52
	speedup miss 100	7.26	7.37
16	read misses	0.093%	0.092%
	write misses	0.0041%	0.0034%
	overall misses	0.071%	0.070%
	invalidations	0.23%	0.23%
	speedup miss 50	14.3	14.5
	speedup miss 100	13.9	14.2
32	read misses	0.12%	0.11%
	write misses	0.010%	0.009%
	overall misses	0.088%	0.085%
	invalidations	0.27%	0.27%
	speedup miss 50	27.5	27.9
	speedup miss 100	26.6	27.1

Table 7.3 Water Simulation Results

invalidations as a fraction of writes; no cold start misses; infinite cache

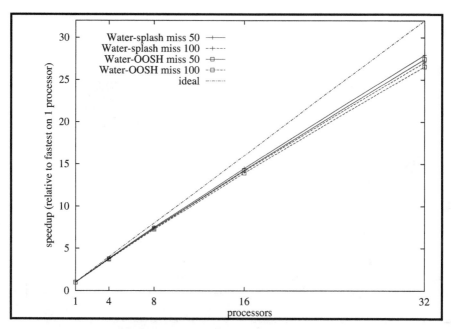

(a) speedups relative to fastest for each cache simulated

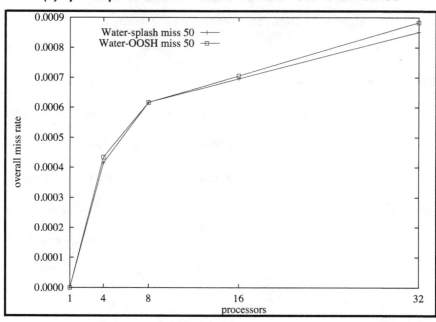

(b) misses (fraction of all references—except cold-start)

Figure 7.3 Simulator Measures for Water
continued on next page

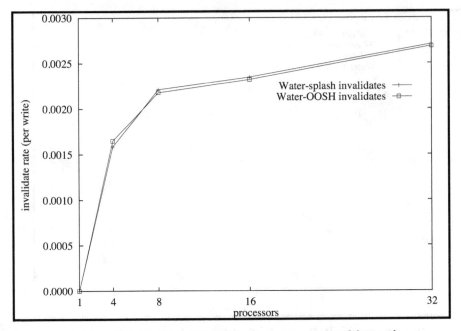

(c) invalidates (fraction of writes — except cold-start)

Figure 7.3 Simulator Measures for Water
continued from previous page

Measurements for Water (table and figure 7.3) are based on the SPLASH data set over 2 steps. However, to increase the amount of work to parallelise, the number of molecules is increased to from 64 to 512 (the number must be a cube).

There is little difference (up to 2% less speed up in the OOSH version), reflecting minimal changes in the OOSH implementation. Restructuring the application would be more worthwhile than trying to optimize such a small difference away.

7.3.2 Real Machine

Times are for SPLASH and OOSH versions of each application, with the exception of MP3D, where the original poorly structured MP3D–0 is once again included. In all cases, runs are on an unloaded machine. Speedup, as with simulated runs, is relative to the fastest uniprocessor run.

MP3D times are with space set up as in the simulation runs, but with times over 1500 steps (1000 steps to reach steady state, counters zeroed, 500 more steps) for consistency with earlier published work [Cheriton *et al*. 1991b]. This is a complete run for this wind tunnel.

The OOSH version is run with both padding and alignment to 64 bytes (the L2 cache block size on the 4D/380) and 4 bytes, to measure the impact of padding and alignment.

Measurements of MP3D runs are presented in table 7.4, and speedup for all

processors	MP3D–0	OOSH			SPLASH
		pad 64	pad 4	pad 4 cost	
1	340 (0.43)	382 (0.38)	389 (0.38)	1.8%	147 (1.0)
2	315 (0.47)	210 (0.70)	219 (0.67)	4.3%	112.6 (1.3)
4	289 (0.51)	122 (1.2)	130 (1.1)	6.6%	94.4 (1.6)
6	318 (0.46)	91.7 (1.6)	99.5 (1.5)	8.5%	97.6 (1.5)
8	352 (0.42)	72.0 (2.0)	84.3 (1.7)	17%	104 (1.4)

Table 7.4 MP3D Run Times
all times in s (speedup relative to fastest, in parentheses)

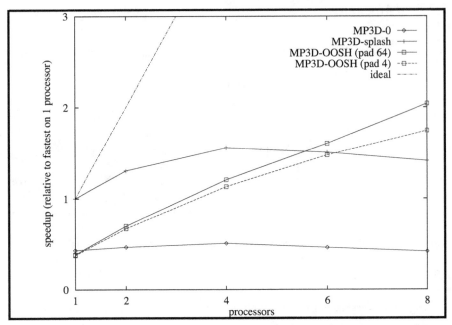

Figure 7.4 Speedup for Runs of MP3D Variations

variations is graphed in figure 7.4.

Run times for Barnes–Hut are based on the SPLASH data set, with 8K particles and 4 time steps. As with MP3D, the OOSH version is run with padding and alignment to both 64 bytes and 4 bytes, to measure the effectiveness of the support for padding and alignment of the OOSH library.

Measured Barnes-Hut run times are in table 7.5, and speedup for all variations is graphed in figure 7.5.

Since OOSH features are not fully used for Water, padding and alignment make no measurable difference, so in this case all runs of the OOSH version are done with padding and alignment to 4 bytes (in effect, there is no padding and alignment— since all data structures are at least 4 bytes in size).

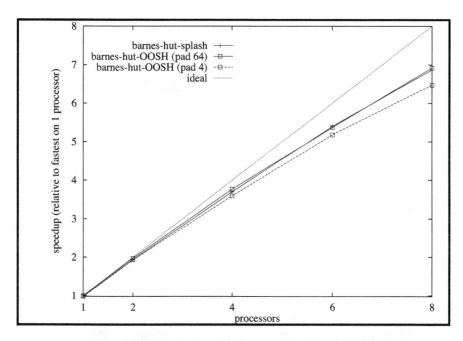

Figure 7.5 Speedup for Barnes-Hut Variations

processors	OOSH			SPLASH
	pad 64	**pad 4**	**pad 4 cost**	
1	101 (1.0)	103 (1.0)	2.0%	102 (1.0)
2	51.2 (2.0)	52.4 (1.9)	2.3%	52.1 (1.9)
4	26.8 (3.8)	28.1 (3.6)	4.9%	27.3 (3.7)
6	18.8 (5.4)	19.5 (5.2)	3.7%	18.7 (5.4)
8	14.6 (6.9)	15.6 (6.5)	6.8%	14.7 (6.9)

Table 7.5 Barnes-Hut Run Times
all times in s (speedup relative to fastest, in parentheses)

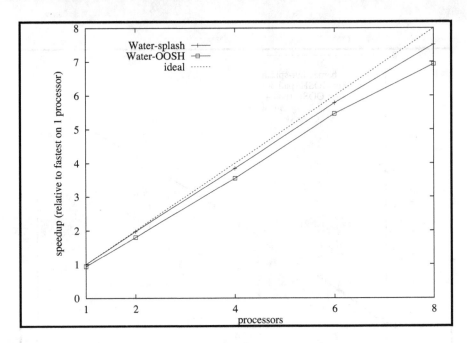

Figure 7.6 Speedup for Water runs
in this case padding and alignment make no measurable difference

Run times and speedup for both versions of Water are summarized in table 7.6,

and speedup is graphed in figure 7.6.

processors	OOSH	SPLASH	OOSH cost
1	74.5 (0.9)	70.0 (1.0)	6.4%
2	38.8 (1.8)	35.4 (2.0)	8.8%
4	19.7 (3.6)	18.2 (3.8)	8.2%
6	12.8 (5.5)	12.1 (5.8)	5.8%
8	10.1 (6.9)	9.32 (7.5)	8.4%

Table 7.6 Water Run Times
all times in s (speedup relative to fastest, in parentheses)

7.3.3 Blocking Measurement of MP3D

There is a relatively large amount of data—since several variations on precinct size are needed for each measure—so data is presented using a different strategy to that of the previous results. All results are presented both as absolute numbers, and as relative to the SPLASH version of MP3D, the better of the two older implementations. Only the relative results are graphed, since the relative results make it possible to compare different measures on similar axes. The absolute results make it possible to check that the derived results make sense.

Since the data set (8000 particles) used in simulations is too small to cause significant L2 misses as a result of replacements on the SGI 4D/380, a bigger example (1-million particles—a more realistic data set) is also used in real machine measurements. To make it possible to do a wide range of measurements in a reasonable amount of time, relatively short runs of each are used: 10 time steps for the large example, and 50 for the small example (even for the real machine runs of the small example).

Precinct sizes are varied from the smallest possible (1 cell high by 1 cell long), to a size big enough to show the extra misses caused when there is no blocking effect. Sizes between are chosen to give a good spread of sizes, especially well below the L1 cache size of 64K on the real machine for both examples, and above and below the L2 cache size for the big example. In all variants, a precinct is the full width of the wind tunnel, since otherwise the number of neighbours that must be taken into account when doing synchronization increases from a maximum of 8 to 26 (when neighbours on all sides must be considered, not just in two dimensions).

	1 processor		4 processors		8 processors	
	run time (s)	OOSH SPLASH	run time (s)	OOSH SPLASH	run time (s)	OOSH SPLASH
SPLASH	*121.4*		*44.26*		*41.39*	
precinct size (K)						
5.56	232.18	1.91	64.87	1.47	39.81	0.96
10.50	222.97	1.84	62.46	1.41	37.87	0.91
20.25	222.04	1.83	62.54	1.41	38.00	0.92
30.00	221.90	1.83	62.82	1.42	38.59	0.93
39.81	221.28	1.82	62.13	1.40	38.49	0.93
44.75	219.25	1.81	62.39	1.41	37.51	0.91
59.44	228.17	1.88	62.22	1.41	38.30	0.93
79.00	221.99	1.83	62.07	1.40	38.01	0.92
97.00	220.82	1.82	62.05	1.40	38.50	0.93
119.19	220.56	1.82	61.34	1.39	37.39	0.90
145.25	218.71	1.80	61.97	1.40	37.77	0.91
177.00	219.42	1.81	61.70	1.39	37.47	0.91
205.25	220.30	1.81	61.59	1.39	37.51	0.91
238.06	219.02	1.80	61.39	1.39	37.66	0.91
267.63	219.38	1.81	61.70	1.39	37.79	0.91
368.25	221.63	1.83	62.88	1.42	38.07	0.92
735.81	220.44	1.82	62.89	1.42	39.46	0.95
1749.94	225.09	1.85	64.86	1.47	39.94	0.96
6006.88 (5.9M)	221.52	1.82	71.55	1.62	52.82	1.28

Table 7.7 Blocked Run Times: 1-Million Particles

all runs over 10 time steps; for each variant in number of processors and precinct size times are also given relative to the SPLASH run time on that number of processors; the OOSH/SPLASH ratios make it possible to compare the benefits of the library versus the SPLASH implementation across variations of number of processors and precinct size, by graphing the OOSH/SPLASH ratios on the same scale

The precinct size in all cases is computed based on the objects used to store the precinct itself, the average number of particles per cell, the size of a cell, the number of cells per precinct and the objects needed to keep track of 8 neighbours of a given precinct. On this basis, the largest possible precinct size (allowing for as few as 8 precincts, to make an 8-processor run possible) for the small example is 142K—less than the L2 cache size of 256K per processor on the SGI 4D/380. By contrast, the largest possible precinct size for the big example, again allowing up to 8 processors, is nearly 12Mbytes (the largest actual example used for the 1-million particle case, in terms of precinct size, uses 16 precincts, each just under 6Mbytes).

Table and figure 7.7 present run times on the large example. The speed variations in the 1-processor case within the precinct sizes which are smaller than either the L1 or L2 cache are interesting to compare with the speed variations found by Lam et al. [1991] for a blocked matrix multiply. In the case of MP3D-OOSH, the difference (expressed as a fraction of the bigger run time) between the smallest (218.71s) and biggest (232.18s) run time is only 5.8%.

For the matrix multiply example (on a DECstation 3100, with a memory system of the same era as the 4D/380), the difference between the best and worst blocked run time is over 50%. One possible explanation for this difference is that conflict

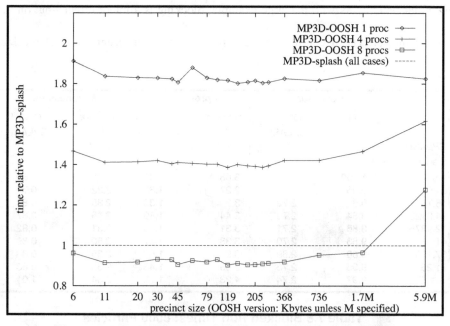

Figure 7.7 Run Times for MP3D with 1-Million Particles

times are relative to the run time for MP3D-SPLASH on the same number of processors; see Table 7.7 for an explanation of presentation strategy

misses, potentially a major problem with sequential array accesses, appear to be less of a factor with relatively randomly allocated data (as in the OOSH implementation). On the other hand, it should be noted that the blocking effect is much less significant than for the matrix multiply: the extra overhead of managing more precincts generally offsets the advantage of blocking. For a multiprocessor run, however, being able to schedule work in finer-grained units improves run times for smaller precincts. On the 8-processor example, provided there are sufficient precincts to schedule work efficiently, the OOSH version is faster than the SPLASH version.

Table and figure 7.8 contain run times for the smaller example. Figure 7.8 also contains simulated run time data for direct comparison: note that when reduced to a ratio between the SPLASH and OOSH versions, the real and simulated times follow a similar pattern. As with the large example, blocking is a minor effect—but on the other hand, effects of conflict misses appear to be insignificant for most precinct sizes.

	1 processor		4 processors		8 processors	
	run time (s)	OOSH / SPLASH	run time (s)	OOSH / SPLASH	run time (s)	OOSH / SPLASH
SPLASH	*3.64*		*2.46*		*2.82*	
precinct size (K)						
2.625	11.09	3.05	3.66	1.49	2.51	0.89
8.6875	9.96	2.74	3.27	1.33	2.22	0.79
16.75	9.91	2.72	3.39	1.38	2.35	0.83
24.3125	9.84	2.70	3.44	1.40	2.45	0.87
32.9375	9.86	2.71	3.31	1.35	2.31	0.82
41	9.83	2.70	3.38	1.37	2.50	0.89
57.125	9.80	2.69	3.98	1.62	2.35	0.83
71.25	9.95	2.73	3.65	1.48	2.33	0.83
141.875	9.97	2.74	4.23	1.72	2.84	1.01

Table 7.8 Blocked Run Times: 8000 Particles

all runs over 50 time steps; see Table 7.7 for explanation of presentation strategy

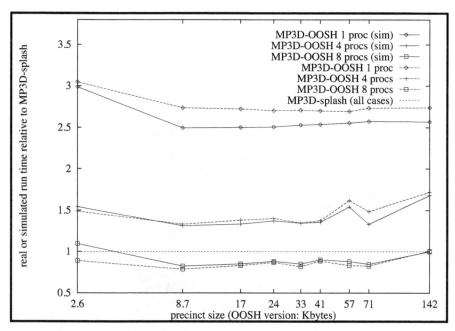

Figure 7.8 Simulated and Real MP3D Times

times are relative to the run time for MP3D-SPLASH on the same number of processors; see Table 7.7 for an explanation of the presentation strategy

Table 7.9 contains simulated measures. Note that in each case, the measure for SPLASH is presented at the top, in italics. Ratios of OOSH measures to SPLASH measures are less than 1 if OOSH is better (faster, fewer misses, etc.).

	1 processor			4 processors			8 processors	
	references	OOSH / SPLASH		references	OOSH / SPLASH		references	OOSH / SPLASH
SPLASH	*26524038*			*26567647*			*26641965*	
precinct size (K)								
2.625	81962242	3.09		86632247	3.26		110858110	4.16
8.6875	77630278	2.93		84965952	3.20		106270927	3.99
16.75	76924697	2.90		86422334	3.25		121448710	4.556
24.3125	76716551	2.89		85110997	3.20		120974790	4.54
32.9375	76456533	2.88		86979561	3.27		112049040	4.21
41	76429473	2.88		89602611	3.37		128936130	4.84
57.125	76319925	2.88		113506607	4.27		145834771	5.47
71.25	76148686	2.87		91476962	3.44		137039679	5.14
141.875	76165534	2.87		138019475	5.20		148663130	5.58

(b) references

	1 processor			4 processors			8 processors	
	cycles	OOSH / SPLASH		cycles	OOSH / SPLASH		cycles	OOSH / SPLASH
SPLASH	*129427608*			*72162060*			*76480266*	
precinct size (K)								
2.625	386602668	2.99		111337984	1.54		83731455	1.09
8.6875	322716702	2.49		94573386	1.31		63087655	0.82
16.75	323507800	2.50		96143151	1.33		65101160	0.85
24.3125	324158033	2.50		98861102	1.37		67522378	0.88
32.9375	327383737	2.53		96889513	1.34		65111004	0.85
41	328238537	2.54		97833956	1.36		69021910	0.90
57.125	330535920	2.55		111204900	1.54		67284419	0.88
71.25	333013301	2.57		95936317	1.33		64911521	0.85
141.875	332459430	2.57		121278859	1.68		76327032	1.00

(a) simulated time in clock cycles

Table 7.9 8000 Particles Blocked Simulation Runs

continued on next page

	1 processor		4 processors		8 processors	
	misses	OOSH / SPLASH	misses	OOSH / SPLASH	misses	OOSH / SPLASH
SPLASH	*441685*		*772746*		*825355*	
precinct size (K)						
2.625	1612852	3.65	1711187	2.21	1890274	2.29
8.6875	1107434	2.51	1268406	1.64	1326091	1.61
16.75	1119985	2.54	1282936	1.66	1323294	1.60
24.3125	1125635	2.55	1395376	1.81	1430536	1.73
32.9375	1157923	2.62	1305845	1.69	1400500	1.70
41	1161265	2.63	1291416	1.67	1426570	1.73
57.125	1179587	2.67	1340921	1.74	1225718	1.49
71.25	1202606	2.72	1225754	1.59	1196443	1.45
141.875	1194226	2.70	1212647	1.57	1200099	1.45

(c) misses

	4 processors		8 processors	
	invalidations	OOSH invals / SPLASH invals	invalidations	OOSH invals / SPLASH invals
SPLASH	*442899*		*536392*	
precinct size (K)				
2.625	14265	0.032	30579	0.057
8.6875	16019	0.036	30014	0.056
16.75	16233	0.037	27501	0.051
24.3125	15564	0.035	25811	0.048
32.9375	14355	0.032	25636	0.048
41	16084	0.036	24579	0.046
57.125	12495	0.028	25313	0.047
71.25	14981	0.034	24604	0.046
141.875	11677	0.026	21316	0.040

(d) invalidations (only occur in multiprocessor runs)

Table 7.9 8000 Particles Blocked Simulation Runs

continued on next page

	1 processor		4 processors		8 processors	
	write backs	OOSH / SPLASH	write backs	OOSH / SPLASH	write backs	OOSH / SPLASH
SPLASH	*418926*		*474416*		*538923*	
precinct size (K)						
2.625	787611	1.88	320225	0.67	63533	0.12
8.6875	683826	1.63	331558	0.70	91788	0.17
16.75	709632	1.69	344820	0.73	108718	0.20
24.3125	722785	1.73	335910	0.71	94778	0.18
32.9375	737122	1.76	342740	0.72	85115	0.16
41	751179	1.79	353991	0.75	107227	0.20
57.125	768829	1.84	382360	0.81	157292	0.29
71.25	783320	1.87	358743	0.76	149757	0.28
141.875	788836	1.88	447786	0.94	204969	0.38

(e) write backs

Table 7.9 8000 Particles Blocked Simulation Runs
...*continued from previous page: 64K direct-mapped simulated cache; see Table 7.7 for explanation of presentation strategy*

Figure 7.9 presents references and misses on one graph. Figure 7.10 presents

invalidations, and figure 7.11 presents write backs. All graphs present data relative to

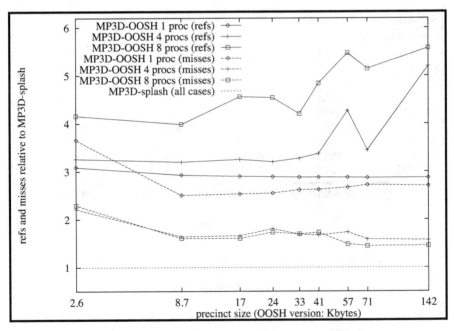

Figure 7.9 References and Misses for MP3D
measures are relative to run time for MP3D-SPLASH on same number of processors; see Table 7.7 for explanation of presentation strategy

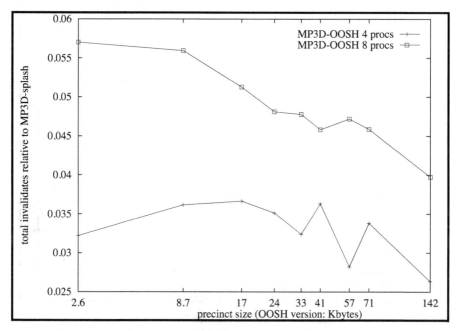

Figure 7.10 Invalidations for MP3D

measures are relative to the run time for MP3D-SPLASH on the same number of processors; see Table 7.7 for an explanation of the presentation strategy

MP3D-SPLASH on the same number of processors.

Figure 7.9 shows some blocking effect in that misses on one processor are lower for most precinct sizes smaller than the simulated cache size of 64K. At the same time, the number of references in the 1-processor case does not vary significantly with precinct size (see table 7.9b for the actual number of references). The maximum variation in number of references is 7%; if the smallest precinct size is excluded, the maximum variation is under 2%. Misses show more variation on one processor: 31%. Again, excluding the smallest precinct reduces the variation, this time to under 8%.

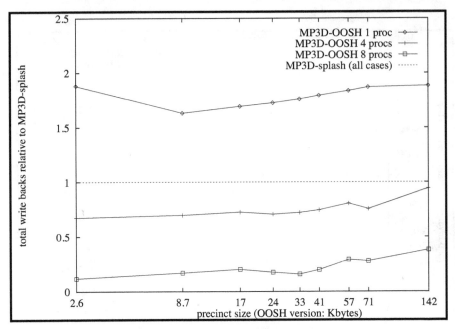

Figure 7.11 Write Backs for MP3D

*measures are relative to the run time for MP3D-SPLASH on the same
number of processors; see Table 7.7 for an explanation of the
presentation strategy*

The multiprocessor cases are more complex. The steep increase in references in
the 4 and 8 processor cases as precinct sized increases—especially for the 57K
precinct—suggests that effects such as load balance and accessing data structures for
synchronization become important factors. Looking at the actual measured values in
table 7.9, it is evident that while MP3D-OOSH has a lower miss ratio than MP3D-
SPLASH, the absolute numbers of references and misses for the library
implementation are higher. As the number of processors increases, the number of
misses in the OOSH version tends to improve relative to the SPLASH version.

Tables 7.9d (invalidations) and 7.9e (write backs) illustrate where MP3D-OOSH
does have a gain over MP3D-SPLASH, which begins to show up in the 8-processor

runs. The number of invalidations on the OOSH version is under 5% those for the SPLASH version for most cases. Invalidations are an important measure of scalability, because an invalidation causes overhead on at least two processors (the one which does the invalidation, by attempting to write a block, and any others that previously shared the block). However, not too much can be read into measures of invalidations here: the absolute numbers are small (especially for OOSH), and any change in reference behaviour in which a shared block is written back or replaced before another processor writes it will reduce invalidations.

A reduction in write backs is a measure of the effectiveness of a blocking strategy. Any block which may be written early in a computation and also at a later stage will be written back more than once if the computation is not effectively blocked. In the multiprocessor case, some write backs are caused by invalidations. However, the number of invalidations is small compared with write backs. Also, the biggest variation in write backs occurs when the 4 and 8 processor runs' precinct size increases to close to or bigger than the simulated cache size of 64K. The smallest precinct generally has a high number of references, misses and write backs — probably because of too much precinct overhead in relation to particle data. Considering only the precincts larger than the smallest one, in the best case (the second-smallest precinct), there are over 13% fewer write backs than in the worst case (the biggest precinct) in the uniprocessor case. The pattern is less clear for the multiprocessor cases, except there is a general tendency for write backs to increase as precinct size increases.

7.4 Interpretation

This section further highlights significant points of the results, followed by a discussion of the impact of restructuring an inefficient application, cleaning up an efficient application, and finally, the performance impact of OOSH constructs on unstructured code.

7.4.1 Significant Points

Each application is considered in turn; results from simulation are used to predict real machine performance, and these predictions are compared with those measured on the 8-processor Silicon Graphics system.

Infinite cache simulation measurement of MP3D indicates that real run times should be significantly different across implementations. Also, the OOSH version should be a lot less sensitive to an increase in cache miss cost than the other two versions. MP3D–0 should give very little if any speedup on any modern shared-memory design.

As predicted by simulation, MP3D–0 achieves very little speedup on the real machine. The SPLASH version, despite removing false sharing and improving prefetch by clustering particle moves, does not speed up on more than 4 processors. The improvement in prefetch and reduction of overhead of parallel constructs make it significantly faster than the other versions on 1 processor. Even without padding and aligning to the block size of the SGI 4D/380, the OOSH version is faster than the SPLASH version on 8 processors. With padding and alignment to 64-byte boundaries, the OOSH version is faster than the SPLASH version on 6 processors as well. The padding and alignment increasingly pays off as the number of processors increases, particularly in the move from 6 to 8 processors, where the percentage performance hit for not padding doubles from 8.5% to 17%.

On 8 processors, the padded aligned OOSH version is just over 30% faster than the SPLASH version, despite the fact that the SPLASH version is 2.6 times faster on a single processor.

Aside from overhead of distributed synchronization, the OOSH version has additional overhead of randomizing collisions. The routine to randomize particle queues alone accounts for 17% of execution time as determined by using the pixie profiling system; other overhead including checking particle time stamps is difficult to measure directly. Extra overhead of the OOSH rewrite can be seen as a trade-off for the greater memory contention of the strategy of MP3D–0 and SPLASH, which use cells to randomly pair collision partners.

Finite cache measurement of MP3D — and the small and large examples on the SGI 4D/380 — show that blocking is a relatively minor effect compared with the other improvements on earlier versions of MP3D. However, unlike with blocked matrix algorithms, it appears that conflict misses are relatively unlikely to cause an increase in misses for specific block sizes.

Barnes-Hut clearly gains from the OOSH implementation, especially on the simulation of the slower memory hierarchy. With a miss cost of 50 cycles, the speed difference between the two implementations is significantly smaller than for the miss cost 100 simulation. The difference is smaller on the real machine run times, where the difference between the pad 64 OOSH and SPLASH run times is under 2% in all cases. This reflects the fact that the real machine is not a recent model (i.e., misses on it cost less than 50 cycles). It should also be noted that the gain from padding and alignment on the real machine—which increases with number of processors as should be expected—is nearly 7% on 8 processors.

The simulation runs of Water predict that run times on the real machine should differ by about 2%. However, in this case, the real machine run times differ by more than the predicted amount—ranging from 5.8% to 8.8%. Examination of profiles of the SPLASH and OOSH version reveals that most of the higher execution time is caused by the extra level of indirection needed to access per-processor globals. The OOSH version accesses per-processor globals through an object, whereas the SPLASH version relies on fork semantics to make private copies of globals.

7.4.2 Restructuring

The benefit to be had from restructuring depends on how poorly the original application is structured.

In the case of MP3D, where speedup of the original version is negligible, effort to find a better overall application structure is justified. Making relatively straightforward changes as in the SPLASH version is not sufficient if the amount of communication is high. As processors become faster in relation to memory hierarchies, this point will become even clearer. On 32 processors, MP3D–0 has an overall miss ratio of 31%. In the SPLASH version, overall misses are improved to 6.4%. Even so, speedup on 32 processors with a miss cost of 100 CPU cycles for the SPLASH version is only 2.4. The OOSH version, with a miss ratio of 0.21%, has a speedup of 5.5 on the same simulated architecture. While considerably better than the other two versions, the OOSH speedup is compromised by the high cost of emulating the random collision pairing semantics of the other programs. A rewrite of MP3D using deeper knowledge of the underlying physics would probably give better results. However, it would be more difficult to compare such a rewrite meaningfully with earlier versions.

Blocking does not give as much of an improvement in MP3D as could be hoped for, based on claimed improvements resulting from blocking of a matrix multiply algorithm [Lam *et al.* 1991]. The major reason for MP3D gaining less from blocking than a matrix multiply does is that there are only two parts of the algorithm in which a particle is referenced, which are combined: move and collide. By contrast, in a matrix multiply (assuming multiplying two NxN matrices), a single element is used in N different computations. However, since blocking of relatively unstructured memory access appears to be less likely to result in conflict misses than is the case with a regularly structured matrix algorithm, blocking is worth doing even for a relatively small gain. Where data is referenced repeatedly in different parts of an algorithm, blocking will be a bigger win.

The rewrite of Barnes-Hut is much closer to the original structure of the program, to the extent that it is possible to compare run times of parts of the code at a fairly detailed level using a profiler. Almost all the Barnes-Hut performance improvement is a result of better cache block-aligned memory allocation.

7.4.3 Cleaning Up

Barnes-Hut illustrates the benefits of cleaning up an existing reasonably well-structured program.

The OOSH implementation has little difference in performance from the SPLASH version on the real machine, or on the simulated machine with a miss cost of 50 cycles. However, on the miss cost 100 simulated machine, speedup of the OOSH version on 32 processors is 27, which is over 20% better than for the SPLASH version's speedup of 22.

The improvement results from the drop in false sharing, as measured by the reduction in misses and invalidations. Again on 32 processors, the SPLASH version has more than twice as many invalidations per write than the OOSH version; the OOSH version has nearly 3 times fewer misses, measured as a fraction of all references.

The miss ratio is relatively low in Barnes-Hut: on 32 processors, the SPLASH version's miss ratio is 0.084%; the OOSH version's miss ratio is 0.031%. Even with such low miss rates, higher memory hierarchy costs will make padding and alignment worthwhile in the near future if current trends continue.

7.4.4 Minimum Overhead

The OOSH Water implementation has a performance loss of up to 9% over the SPLASH version, as measured on the real machine. This can be considered an upper bound on the cost of OOSH for an application of this nature, since no effort has been made at optimization. The real loss is higher than the 2% overhead predicted by simulation.

Water has similar miss ratios to the OOSH version of Barnes-Hut, though the fraction of invalidations is substantially higher (3.5 times higher on 32 processors). If similar improvements to those achieved for Barnes-Hut could be made, it would be worth the effort of reimplementing Water using OOSH more fully.

7.5 Overall Findings

The biggest benefit from the library is seen from completely rewriting MP3D. MP3D is a soft target since it has extremely poor cache behaviour, even in the modestly restructured SPLASH version.

Barnes-Hut, which is already reasonably well optimized, is a more convincing demonstration of the value of OOSH. Although the improvements affected by using the library could be achieved by an ad hoc strategy of padding and aligning, OOSH makes it possible to reuse the cache block sensitive low-level memory allocators. An improvement of about 20% in performance is predicted on a 32-processor run on a machine with a miss cost of 100 clock cycles, which is significant especially as the overall structure of the code is little changed.

Water illustrates that the overhead of OOSH can be relatively high if no attempt is made at optimizing for it or making good use of its features. Clearly, any performance-oriented programmer would make such an attempt at optimizing, whatever the underlying strategy or tools being used. A reusable object-oriented library should in principle allow the programmer to focus on algorithmic improvements, without having to spend a lot of time on architecture-specific detail, such as the impact of cache block size.

Commentary

In a multicore architecture, the effect of cache invalidations may be less of a bottleneck than with the architectures studied here particularly if a shared lower-level cache captures all the shared references. Even so, false sharing is an unnecessary extra overhead that may limit speedup.

Memory structuring such as blocking on the other hand may make an even bigger difference over a decade on from the original work. Despite the slowdown in clock speed enhancement and the ratcheting back from multiple instructions per clock, a multicore design at 3GHz is nearly 100 times faster in clock speed than machines of the first half of the 1990s, while DRAM speed has advanced nowhere near as fast.

---

8. Conclusions

8.1 Introduction

This chapter summarizes the research and places it in context.

Potential future work is presented to illustrate potential for expanding and continuing the research, followed by an analysis of results and a summary of the contribution made by this work.

Some of the alternative synchronization strategies described in Chapter 3 could be adapted to OOSH. Since such adaptation would be fairly straightforward in most cases, this chapter does not take the issue further.

Another area where more work could be useful—now that the ANSI C++ standard has begun to stabilize—is in tidying up the implementation and investigating the use of language features that were in the process of being implemented when this research was started, including templates and exceptions. Most compilers have these features now, though some details were still under discussion as this work was concluded. Since this is a matter of implementation detail, it is also not discussed further.

Future work which is considered in more detail is broken down into issues for interacting with paging strategies, and issues for slower memory hierarchies, based on research in the area of distributed shared memory.

Paging strategies are important because large memory systems result in more overhead in page address translation even if there are no page faults [Huck and Hays 1993], and application structuring in future may need to take such effects into account.

A distributed shared memory architecture is logically a shared memory architecture but is implemented on a number of networked systems, and typically uses units of a page to transfer data (because of the latency of networks compared with traditional multiprocessor interconnects).

8.2 Future Work

The work reported on here focuses on cache issues; other parts of the memory hierarchy can also play a significant role in performance. Also, as cache miss costs increase, there should be a growing convergence between issues in conventional shared memory architectures and in distributed shared memory architectures. This section examines potential future work which would take into account the virtual memory system, followed by possible extensions to take into account issues in distributed shared memory. Obviously, it would also be desirable to do detailed optimization of both the library and specific applications, to further reduce overheads (especially in the case of MP3D).

Although such applications are not considered here, it should also be noted that another area for future work is investigating the applicability of techniques developed in this research to a wider range of problem areas. Although OOSH is designed for time-stepped simulation, much of the code could be adapted to other purposes, especially the memory allocators.

8.2.1 Virtual Memory Issues

As early as the 1970s, there was work on restructuring programs for good performance in paged virtual memory systems [Ferrari 1976, Hatfield and Gerald 1971, Snyder 1978, Spirn 1977].

A modern paged virtual memory system with page cache management outside the kernel offers possibilities for designing page replacement strategies tuned to a specific application [Harty and Cheriton 1991; Subramanian 1991].

A related issue—discovered as a side-effect of this research—is the potential mismatch between object-oriented code and translation lookaside buffers. A TLB is a small cache of recent page translations, which relies heavily on spatial locality to give good performance. A small TLB with 32 entries each mapping a 4K page may have few misses with code referencing approximately sequential addresses (as in typical vector or matrix processing). However, if objects are allocated without attempting to keep those accessed at roughly the same time close in memory, a high number of TLB misses may result especially with a small TLB. A study of this problem with the MP3D application has revealed that TLB misses could account for an increase of as much as 25% in run time in a run with randomly allocated objects, as compared with a run with contiguously allocated objects.

Figure 8.1 illustrates how on a large 8-processor run, MP3D has an increasing number of TLB misses on a Silicon Graphics 4D/380. The run is on a wind tunnel

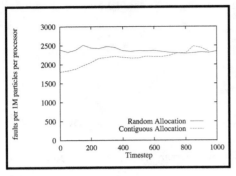
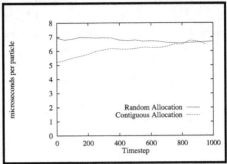

(a) TLB misses per
processor per timestep

(b) execution time per
particle per timestep

Figure 8.1 TLB Effects in Large MP3D Run

with 131 by 131 by 7 cells, and 1-million particles. Initially, particles are allocated contiguously within cells. As they move through space, particles close in space gradually cease to be close in memory.

Figure 8.1a shows how the number of TLB misses increases with time for a run with particles initially contiguously allocated until—after around 800 time steps—the number of misses is about the same as for a run with particles initially randomly allocated. Figure 8.1b shows how this effect impacts performance.

In an application like MP3D (or to a lesser extent Barnes-Hut, where movement of bodies is slower), this is a difficult problem to solve. Copying data as it moves through the simulation to keep it contiguous can be as expensive as the TLB misses, as each additional copy can potentially result in a cache miss [Cheriton *et al*. 1993].

Adding user-level page replacement could be a solution to the TLB miss problem. If data that moves in the simulation (particles in the case of MP3D; bodies in Barnes-Hut) is allocated a page at a time, when a page is moved from being

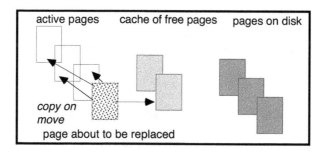

Figure 8.2 Copy on Move
to allow deallocation on page replacement

memory resident to being cached, its contents could be copied to free memory

belonging to the part of the simulation the object has moved to. The old page would

be marked as garbage for a garbage collector. Some limit is needed, to ensure that

thrashing does not occur. For example, reallocation can only be done as long it does

not lead to a miss to disk.

Another possibility would be to exploit the fact that the simulation is set up with

a mean free path of about a third of a cell, so in about 5 timesteps, there is a high

probability that all particles will have left a given cell. If each cell reallocates

particles on arrival and uses a simple scheme to keep track of the range of addresses

currently in use, a simple page replacement-based garbage collector could be

implemented. Reallocation would still be expensive, but the cost of appending

deleted data objects to a free list would be eliminated. The viability of this strategy

depends on a number of issues including the relative costs of TLB misses and cache

misses.

Figure 8.2 illustrates the idea.

8.2.2 Slower Memory Hierarchies

One of the most important strategies for reducing the cost of misses on distributed shared memory systems is weaker models of consistency. For example, *release consistency* assumes that all shared data structures that are written are protected by a lock. When a lock is released, consistency must be ensured, but while the lock is still held, it is assumed that other processors that would have referenced the shared data will not see an inconsistent copy since they should be blocked by the lock [Gharachorloo *et al.* 1990].

Release consistency has been used not only in distributed shared memory systems [Dwarkadas *et al.* 1993] but in the DASH system [Lenoski *et al.* 1992]. In fact the DASH designers did much of the early work in this area.

Future shared memory multiprocessor systems with higher memory latencies will increasingly need to use techniques such as release consistency .

The aligned memory allocators used for OOSH are highly suited to release consistency. If a lock is to protect not only a logical data structure but all data structures contained within a given group of blocks, it is essential that there be no false sharing.

Padding and aligning to blocks as big as typical page sizes (4K or 8Kbytes, though recent architectures such as the MIPS R4000 support much larger sizes) is not practical, so techniques to aggregate blocks of related data will become increasingly important. Implementation of such memory management strategies at a low level as part of a memory allocator is clearly a superior strategy to ad hoc approaches, which are likely to result in considerable rewriting of code as architecture trade-offs change.

Since distributed shared memory systems usually transfer pages on cache misses, strategies such as release consistency would have to be addressed for a DSM version of OOSH.

8.3 Analysis of Results

For current architectures with low miss costs, the performance benefit of restructuring applications which already have low miss rates is marginal. The extra cost of object-oriented code is partially offset by gains from reduced cache misses, but the difference is big enough to justify writing new code in the OOSH style.

However, simulation results for architectures in which cache miss costs are higher show the value of restructuring using OOSH. Already, high-end systems have higher miss costs than the higher number used in measurement here.

Applications that are reasonably close to object-oriented in style—such as Barnes-Hut—are already worth porting to OOSH, assuming no unexpected breakthrough in memory system performance. Applications with more complex or less well-documented data structures are more difficult to port. Users of such software may eventually be forced to choose between rewriting their code completely, or staying with relatively special-purpose architectures with expensive memory systems, such as vector machines—if current trends continue.

Another effect that has been found to be relatively insignificant in this research is blocking of object-oriented code. Even the relatively small decreases in misses of around 5 to 10% seen here may become important as the memory-processor speed gap grows.

The designers of COOL consider it acceptable that their language imposes a penalty of 2 to 3% as a cost for a simpler programming model [Chandra *et al.* 1994]. OOSH has a cost of this order if its performance enhancing features are not used, as seen from the Water simulation results, or up to 9% as measured on the real machine. For MP3D and Barnes-Hut, with a miss cost of only 100 cycles, performance improvement of about 56% and 18% respectively are predicted by simulation.

In the longer term, the techniques described here may not be sufficient and more heed will need to be taken of structuring techniques used in distributed shared memory systems and even distributed memory systems.

However, OOSH provides a basis on which changes in low-level allocation strategy can be accommodated, and well-designed object-oriented code should in principle be easier to modify for future strategies. For example, it may become necessary to change the data so that parts that are written in one phase of the computation are separate from parts that are read only. Properly designed object-oriented code does not make the representation visible to the whole program, so such a change would be easier to achieve than with a C or FORTRAN implementation.

8.4 Original Contribution

This research demonstrates that an object-oriented library written in C++, while introducing overhead compared with programming directly in C, has advantages for introducing architecture-specific memory allocators. A C++ library also provides a basis for reusing code to support blocking of relatively unstructured data (as compared with arrays).

The research also demonstrates that a relatively disciplined style of code, in which machine dependencies are restricted to a small module, is not an obstacle to good performance. On the contrary, such an approach lends itself to changing machine-specific code for future architectures. As proposed in the future research section of this chapter, this machine-specific code could be adapted for relaxed consistency models typical of distributed shared memory systems and user-level page replacement.

Finally, the utility of the library is demonstrated by showing that it can result in significant performance improvements on future-generation systems with high memory hierarchy costs. For an application which is already well structured—Barnes Hut—the improved memory allocation strategy of OOSH is shown to give a performance improvement of more than 20% over the SPLASH version, on a simulated 32-processor machine with a cache miss cost of 100 clock cycles.

Object blocking, while relatively insignificant compared with the gains of better memory allocation and processor affinity, is likely to become important as miss costs continue to rise. Also, for applications where repeated references to the same object occur in many different places, object blocking is likely to be a bigger win than is the case for MP3D.

Commentary

The role of the TLB in performance remains important and often neglected. If you didn't understand it, go back and try again. In many applications, it can be more significant than cache misses.

A significant category of application in which TLB misses can play a major role is databases which are often not, as one may think, disk-limited but memory system performance limited. **Exercise for the reader**: do a literature search on the keywords: "TLB database performance".

Appendix A MP3D History

As a consequence of its poor cache behaviour, MP3D has been restructured several times. The earliest shared-memory version was based closely on the original vector code [McDonald and Baganoff 1988], and was implemented by Jeff McDonald on an Encore Multimax, a machine with relatively slow processors in relation to memory speed.

It is useful to chronicle earlier versions here because they are referred to in earlier published work. Versions used in this research are MP3D-0, the Multimax version with minor changes to pass the stricter type checks of a C++ compiler, the OOSH version, and the SPLASH version—which are described in Chapter 6.

In work leading up to this research, three versions of MP3D were implemented:

MP3D-1 particle arrays were combined into arrays of objects—this is much the same data structure reorganization as was carried out in the SPLASH version, but without the division of the particle array between processors

MP3D-2 spatial locality in the wind tunnel was made explicit in the program by introducing precincts as units of work allocation, where a precinct was a fixed unit of space; precincts were allocated statically and there was one per processor

MP3D–3 this prototype of the OOSH version was used to study distributed

synchronization and TLB effects [Cheriton *et al*. 1993], as well as to

design the feature set of OOSH

Appendix B Architecture Simulation

B.1 Introduction

The simulator is based on a simple infinite cache back-end supplied as an example with Mint, implemented by C code in files cache.c and bus.c.

A few changes have been made to Mint for correct sproc semantics (launch a new process in the same address space) but those changes are bug fixes rather than substantial changes and are not reported here. Another minor change is addition of a report of elapsed simulated CPU cycles and simulated time when the first new process is launched – useful to factor out initialization.

Of more significance is the handling of memory references. The provided code counts hits and misses. A few changes have been made to record more statistics, and to record cold start misses so they can be factored out.

The purpose of this research is to predict performance of applications created using OOSH rather than to design a new architecture, so simulations are kept simple. This appendix goes on to provide a few details of the memory system and the bus, and explains the impact of approximations on the measured advantages of OOSH.

B.2 Memory System

The Mint backend handles all reads and writes using a simple event-based mechanism. If the cache contains the necessary data with the tags in a suitable state for the required operation, the read or write handler returns T_ADVANCE, informing the simulator that the event has completed. If it cannot complete (because an invalidation or miss has to be handled), a new event is scheduled for the bus. A bus event has a completion and non-completion routine, one of which is called depending on whether the bus is free when the event is scheduled.

The state transitions for the infinite cache simulations are depicted in figure b.1; the finite cache simulation differs only in introducing replacements.

For the infinite cache simulation, a cache block is modeled as a simple data structure with status bits for each processor. The cache is direct mapped, as associativity is not meaningful in an infinite cache. The finite cache is also direct mapped, and is implemented as an array of tags, one per processor. Since MINT is a direct execution simulator, the data contained in the caches need not be stored; the memory system of the real system contains the actual data.

B.3 Bus And Impact Of Approximations

The bus is loosely based on the Silicon Graphics Challenge design (see Appendix D). It has 5 pipeline stages, and all transactions can be fully pipelined, giving an

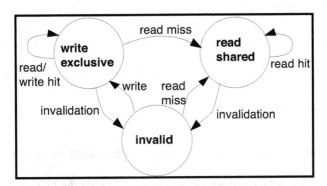

Figure b.1 State Transitions—Infinite Cache

*before state can change to write exclusive an invalidation must be
issued; any transition from write exclusive also includes a write back*

best-case latency of one pipeline stage, though each individual transaction takes 5 stages. This is somewhat more aggressive than a real bus, and favours applications with a high number of misses. On the other hand, an invalidation is treated the same way, which is less aggressive than need be, since a real machine can handle an invalidation without occupying the data bus. The Challenge, for example, can overlap signaling an invalidation on the address bus with a data bus transaction [Galles and Williams 1994].

These approximations nonetheless are good enough for the purpose of this exercise. The only application that is likely to be affected by excessive cost of invalidations in MP3D–0, which has so many misses in any case that it is unlikely to have much speedup on a modern machine (as evidenced by the real machine results). The aggressive handling of misses slightly favours the SPLASH versions of MP3D and Barnes-Hut, but the real machine results show that this inaccuracy is not sufficient to significantly alter the relative rankings of the applications. Since the effect of the inaccuracy is to reduce the advantage of the OOSH versions, it is good enough to establish a lower bound on the claimed improvement.

Furthermore, the measure of most interest is the impact of a change in the relative miss cost of memory operations. These inaccuracies do not seriously affect this change, and again at worst result in a good lower bound.

Appendix C Application Parameters

C.1 Introduction

Application parameters are provided here in sufficient detail to allow repetition of the measurements reported here. In cases where large data files are required, information as to where they can be found is supplied.

There are two FTP sites where data files can be found. Original SPLASH files can be found at

```
ftp://www-flash.stanford.edu/pub/old_splash/splash
```

—referred to as the "SPLASH" site here. Modified files are at the site referred to as "modified" here:

```
ftp://ftp.cs.wits.ac.za/pub/general/programming/research
```

C.2 MP3D

For the small example used in all simulations, the MP3D runs are with a wind tunnel of 20 by 28 by 6 cells, an example provided by original MP3D programmer Jeff McDonald. The wind tunnel is initialized with 8000 particles. The large example used in real machine runs for measuring blocking uses 1-million particles in a wind tunnel of 131 by 131 by 7 cells.

The simulation runs for 50 timesteps; the small example on the real machine runs for 1000 timesteps, after which counters are zeroed and another 500 steps are run. The big example is run for only 10 steps on the real machine, since it has to be

run for a variety of precinct sizes.

A typical session (OOSH version) looks like this:

```
% mp3d 1 64 8000
aligning to cache block size 64
Opened geom file 'space.geom'.
Opened precincts file 'precincts'.
  init particles...No particle file <particles.8000>
generating from scratch.
... particles done.
[mp3d-ds 1] 50
8000 particles Elapsed time for advance : 4s 680000us;
8233 particles 50 steps, 50 cumulative steps.
[mp3d-ds 2] r
Run Status
Number of molecules........8233
Number of steps...........50
Number of Avg. Steps.......50
Upstream MFP ..............1
Free Pop .................10.6383
Gamma.....................1.4
Coll Prob ................0.0025355
Num collisions ...........88
Total collisions..........3477
Num BC ...................28
Num moves (mean) .........8267.9
[mp3d-ds 3] q
```

Command line arguments are number of processors, cache block size and

number of particles.

Commands accepted by the interpreter include

r   report

n   run for n steps (where n is a positive integer)

z   zero counters (used after steady state reached)

q   quit

Other parameters are set in the file space.geom (modified site).

C.3 Barnes-Hut

Barnes-Hut is run with the same parameters as in the SPLASH report: 8K particles for 4 timesteps (real machine and simulations). The data files are at the SPLASH site. The OOSH version (as with MP3D) sets the number of processors in the command line. Otherwise the input file on the SPLASH site works for the OOSH version. The input file is designed for input redirection, to avoid typing in numbers to prompts.

```
A typical run of the OOSH version looks like this:
% barnes 1 64 < splash.in
aligning to cache block size 64
num_bodies 8192
seed 123
step_time 0.025
eps 0.05
tolerance 1
ignore next input 2
stop_time 0.075
data_out 0.25
rejects = 68
```

Command line arguments are number of processors and cache block size.

C.4 Water

Water requires the files in the inputs directory of the SPLASH distribution. Otherwise, it requires a file to be redirected into the program as with Barnes-Hut.

The SPLASH input file is for a 64-particle example. In this case, this number is increased to 512 (real machine and simulations). The input file at the SPLASH site (`sample.in`) is otherwise unchanged; `512.in` at the modified site is the modified input.

An OOSH version run looks like this (command line as for Barnes-Hut):

```
% water 1 64 < sample.in
aligning to cache block size 64
Using 1 procs on 2 steps of 64 mols
Elapsed time for advance : 0s 520000us;
NumProcs 1
```

Appendix D SGI Challenge Miss costs

Miss costs of the Silicon Graphics Challenge multiprocessor's memory hierarchy have not been published, but can be estimated from figures given for the POWERpath-2 bus [Galles and Williams 1994].

The bus has a 21ns cycle, and has a 5-stage pipeline. The bus splits data traffic from addresses and arbitration, in an attempt at minimizing latency. The bus executes the following states system wide: arbitration, resolution, address, decode and acknowledge. The bus is optimized for reads, which can occur in parallel with activity on the address bus.

The most significant aspects of the bus from the point of view of computing miss cost are the time it takes for data to appear after an address is placed on the bus, the number of bus transactions taken to move one cache block and the cache controller overhead to place the block in both L2 and L1 caches.

The first number required—the time before data appears on the bus after a read address appears on the bus—is 12 bus clocks.

The bus is 256 bits wide, and a cache block is 128 bytes. This means that 4 bus cycles are required to move an entire block, once transfer has initiated. The total number of cycles then is 16—not counting arbitration. If arbitration is taken into account, and the bus is unloaded, the total number of bus cycles required to handle a read miss is 18.

The architecture is designed so that read miss handling starts without delay on a cache miss, so there is no additional start up overhead. The overhead to place the block in the cache, copy it to the L1 cache and restart the processor is approximately 600ns[*].

Since each bus cycle is 21ns, the total time to handle a read miss is therefore $18 \times 21\text{ns} + 600\text{ns} \approx 1\mu\text{s}$.

It should be noted that this is the best case for a miss to RAM, since the bus may be busy when the miss occurs. However, other aspects of the design are low in latency. For example, it is possible to transfer data between caches. For these reasons, there is not a single measure of miss latency on this architecture.

The simulated architecture of Appendix B is a simplified version of the Challenge, without some of these optimizations.

---

[*] Source: Dave Olson, Silicon Graphics

References

Some references are superseded by later versions obtainable by FTP. In those cases, a reference in URL format is given for the newer versions.

[Allison 1993] B Allison. DEC 7000/10000 Model 600 AXP Multiprocessor Server, *Proc. IEEE COMPCON*, San Francisco, February 1993, pp 456–464.

[Agrawal and El Abbadi 1991] D Agrawal and A El Abbadi. An Efficient and Fault-Tolerant Solution for Distributed Mutual Exclusion, *ACM Trans. on Computer Systems*, vol. 9 no. 1 February 1991, pp 1–20.

[Agrawal *et al.* 1990] A Agarwal, B-H Lim, D Kranz and J Kubiatowicz. APRIL: A Processor Architecture for Multiprocessing, *Proc. 17th Int. Symp. on Computer Architecture*, Seattle, WA, May 1990, pp 104–114.

[Bacon *et al.* 1994] DF Bacon, SL Graham and OJ Sharp. Compiler Transformations for High-Performance Computing, *ACM Computing Surveys*, vol. 26 no. 4 December 1994, pp 345–420.

[Bakoglu *et al.* 1990] HB Bakoglu, GF Grohoski and RK Montoyne. The IBM RISC System/6000 processor: Hardware Overview, *IBM Journal of Research and Development*, vol. 34 no. 1 January 1990, pp 12–22.

[Barnes and Hut 1986] J Barnes and P Hut. A Hierarchical $O(N \log N)$ Force-Calculation Algorithm, *Nature*, vol. 324 no. 4 December 1986, pp 446–449.

[Beck 1990] B Beck. Shared-Memory Parallel Programming in C++, *IEEE Software*, vol. 7 no. 4 July 1990, pp 38–48.

[Bennet *et al.* 1990] JK Bennet, JB Carter and W Zwaenepoel. Adaptive Software Cache Management for Distributed Shared Memory Architectures, *Proc. 17th Int. Symp. on Computer Architecture*, Seattle, WA, May 1990, pp 125–134.

[Bershad *et al.* 1988] BN Bershad, ED Lazowska and HM Levy. PRESTO: A System for Object-Oriented Parallel Programming, *Software—Practice and Experience*, vol. 18 no. 8 August 1988, pp 713–732.

[Bershad *et al.* 1992] BN Bershad, D Lee, TH Romer and JB Chen. Avoiding Conflict Misses Dynamically in Large Direct-Mapped Caches, *Proc. 6th Int. Conf. on Architectural Support for Programming Languages and Operating Systems*, San Jose, CA, October 1992, pp 158–170.

[Boland and Dollas 1994] K Boland and A Dollas. Predicting and Precluding Problems with Memory Latency, *IEEE Micro*, vol. 14 no. 4 August 1994, pp 59–67.

[Booch 1991] G Booch. *Object-Oriented Design with Applications*, Benjamin/Cummings, Redwood City, CA, 1991.

[Camp *et al.* 1994] WJ Camp, SJ Plimpton, BA Hendrickson and RW Leland. Massively Parallel Methods for Engineering and Science Problems, *Communications of the ACM*, vol. 37 no. 4 April 1994, pp 31–41.

[Cardelli and Wegner 1985] L Cardelli and P Wegner. On Understanding Types, Data Abstraction and Polymorphism, *ACM Computing Surveys*, vol. 17 no. 4 December 1985, pp 471–522.

[Cekleov *et al.* 1993] M Cekleov *et al.*, SPARCcenter 2000: Multiprocessing for the 90s! *Proc. IEEE COMPCON*, San Francisco, February 1993, pp 345–353.

[Chaiken *et al.* 1991] D Chaiken, J Kubiatowicz and A Agarwal. LimitLESS Directories: A Scalable Cache Coherence Scheme, *Proc. 4th Int. Conf. on Architectural Support for Programming Languages and Operating Systems*, Santa Clara, CA, 1991, pp 224–234.

[Chandra *et al.* 1994] R Chandra, A Gupta and JL Hennessy. COOL: An Object-Based Language for Parallel Programming, *Computer*, vol. 27 no. 8 August 1994, pp 13–26.

[Cheriton *et al.* 1991a] DR Cheriton, HA Goosen and PD Boyle. ParaDiGM: A Highly Scalable Shared-Memory Architecture, *Computer*, vol. 24 no. 2 February 1991, pp 33–46.

[Cheriton *et al.* 1991b] DR Cheriton, H A Goosen and P Machanick. Restructuring a Parallel Simulation to Improve Cache Behavior in a Shared-Memory Multiprocessor: A First Experience, *Proc. Int. Symp. on Shared Memory Multiprocessing*, Tokyo, April 1991, pp 109–118.

[Cheriton *et al.* 1993] DR Cheriton, HA Goosen, H Holbrook and P Machanick. Restructuring a Parallel Simulation to Improve Cache Behavior in a Shared-Memory Multiprocessor: The Value of Distributed Synchronization, *Proc. 7th Workshop on Parallel and Distributed Simulation*, San Diego, May 1993, pp 159–162.

[Cheriton *et al.* 1986] DR Cheriton, G Slavenburg and P Boyle. Software-Controlled Caches in the VMP Multiprocessor, *Proc. 13th Int. Symp. on Computer Architecture*, June 1986, pp 366–274.

[Cox 1991] BJ Cox. *Object-Oriented Programming: An Evolutionary Approach* (2nd edition), Addison-Wesley, Reading, MA, 1991.

[Cray 1994] *Technical Overview of the Cray Superserver 6400*, Cray Research Inc., Beaverton, OR, 1994.

[Crowl 1994] Crowl, LA. How to Measure, Present, and Compare Parallel Performance, *IEEE Parallel and Distributed Technology*, vol. 2 no. 1 Spring 1994, pp 9–25.

[Dahl *et al*. 1970] O-J Dahl, B Myrhaug and K Nygaard. *Simula Common Base Language*, Norwegian Computing Centre S–22, Oslow, Norway, 1970.

[Demmel and Higham 1992] JW Demmel and NJ Higham. Stability of Block Algorithms with Fast Level-3 BLAS, *ACM Transactions on Mathematical Software*, vol. 18 no. 3, September 1992, pp 274–291.

[Dener 1992] C Dener. *Development of an Interactive Grid Generation and Geometry Modelling System with Object-Oriented Programming*, PhD Thesis, Dept. of Fluid Mechanics, Vrije Universiteit, Brussels, 1992.

[DoD 1983] *Reference Manual for the Ada® Programming Language*, ANSI/MIL-STD-815A-1983, US Department of Defense, Washington, DC, 1983.

[Dosanjh 1995] SS Dosanjh. Recursive Speedup, *IEEE Computational Science and Engineering*, vol. 2 no. 1 Spring 1995, pp 4–5.

[Dwarkadas *et al*. 1993] S Dwarkadas, P Keleher, AL Cox and W Zwaenepoel. Release Consistent Software Distributed Shared Memory on Emerging Network Technology, *Proc. 20th Int. Symp. on Computer Architecture*, San Diego, CA, May 1993, pp 144–155.

[Eggers and Katz 1989] SJ Eggers and RH Katz. The Effect of Sharing on the Cache and Bus Performance of Parallel Programs, *Proc. 3rd Int. Conf. on Architectural Support for Programming Languages and Operating Systems*, Boston, MA, 1989, pp 257–270.

[Ellis and Stroustrup 1990] MA Ellis and B Stroustrup. *The Annotated C++ Reference Manual*, Addison-Wesley, Reading, MA, 1990.

[Farmwald and Mooring 1992] M Farmwald and D Mooring. A Fast Path to Memory, *IEEE Spectrum*, vol. 29 no. 10 October 1992, pp 50–51.

[Fatoohi 1990] RA Fatoohi. Vector Performance Analysis of the NEC SX-2, *Proc. Int. Conf. on Supercomputing*, Amsterdam, 1990, pp 389–400.

[Ferrari 1976] D Ferrari. The Improvement of Program Behavior, *Computer*, vol. 9 no. 11, November 1976, pp 39–47.

[Forslund *et al*. 1990] DW Forslund, C Wingate, P Ford, JS Junkins, J Jackson and SC Pope. Experiences in Writing a Distributed Particle Simulation Code in C++, *Proc. USENIX C++ Conf.*, 1990, pp 177–190.

[Frailong *et al*. 1993] J-M Frailong, M Cekleov, P Sindhu, J Gastinel, M Splain, J Price and A Singhal. The Next-Generation SPARC Multiprocessing System Architecture, *Proc. IEEE COMPCON*, San Francisco, February 1993, pp 475–480.

[Fujimoto 1990] R Fujimoto. Parallel Discrete Event Simulation, *Communications of the ACM*, vol. 33 no. 10 October 1990, pp 30–53.

[Galles and Williams 1994] M Galles and E Williams. *Performance Optimizations, Implementation, and Verification of the SGI Challenge Multiprocessor*, Silicon Graphics Inc., Mountain View, CA, 1994.

[Gharachorloo *et al.* 1990] K Gharachorloo, D Lenoski, J Laudon, P Gibbons, A Gupta and J Hennessy. Memory Consistency and Event Ordering in Scalable Shared-Memory Multiprocessors, *Proc. 17th Int. Symp. on Computer Architecture*, Seattle, WA, May 1990, pp 15–26.

[Goldberg and Robson 1983] A Goldberg and D Robson. *Smalltalk–80: The Language and its Implementation*, Addison-Wesley, Reading, MA, 1983.

[Goldschmidt and Davis 1990] SR Goldschmidt and H Davis. *Tango Introduction and Tutorial*, Technical Report CSL–TR–90–410, Computer Systems Laboratory, Stanford University, Stanford, CA, 1990.

[Goodman 1987] JR Goodman. Coherency for Multiprocessor Virtual Address Caches, *Proc. 2nd Int. Conf. on Architectural Support for Programming Languages and Operating Systems*, Palo Alto, CA, October 1987, pp 72–81.

[Goosen 1991] HA Goosen. *Shared Multilevel Caches for Scalable Multiprocessors*, Technical Report (PhD thesis) STAN–CS–91–1393, Computer Science Department, Stanford University, October 1991.

[Goosen *et al.* 1993] HA Goosen, AR Karlin and DR Cheriton. Chiron: A System for Parallel Program Visualization, *Proc. Conf. on Advanced Techniques in Animation, Rendering and Visualization*, Ankara, Turkey, July 1993.

[Hagersten *et al.* 1992] E Hagersten, A Landin and S Haridi. DDM—A Cache-Only Memory Architecture, *Computer,* vol. 25 no. 9 September 1992, pp 44–54.

[Haney 1994] SW Haney. Is C++ Fast Enough for Scientific Computing? *Computers in Physics*, vol. 8 no. 6, November/December 1994, pp 690–694.

[Harty and Cheriton 1991] K Harty and DR Cheriton. Application-Controlled Physical Memory Using External Page-Cache Management, Technical Report CS–TR–91–1394, Computer Science Department, Stanford University, October 1991.

[Hatfield and Gerald 1971] D Hatfield and J Gerald. Program Restructuring for Virtual Memory, *IBM Systems Journal*, vol. 10, 1971, pp 168–192.

[Hennessy and Jouppi 1991] JL Hennessy and P Jouppi. Computer Technology and Architecture: An Evolving Interaction, *Computer*, vol. 24 no. 9, September, 1991, pp 18–29.

[Hennessy and Patterson 1995] JL Hennessy and DA Patterson. *Computer Architecture: A Quantitative Approach* (2nd edition), Morgan Kaufman, San Mateo, 1995.

[Hsu 1994] P Y-T Hsu. *Design of the R8000 Microprocessor*, MIPS Technologies, Inc., Mountain View, CA, 1994.

[Huck and Hays 1993] J Huck and J Hays. Architectural Support for Translation Table Management in Large Address Spaces, *Proc. 20th Int. Symp. on Computer Architecture*, San Diego, CA, May 1993, pp 39–50.

[Hwang *et al*. 1995] Y-S Hwang, R Das, JH Saltz, M Hodoscek and BR Brooks. Parallelizing Molecular Dynamics Programs for Distributed-Memory Machines, *IEEE Computational Science and Engineering*, vol. 2 no. 2, Summer 1995, pp 18–29.

[Inouye *et al*. 1992] J Inouye, R Konuru, J Walpole and B Sears. The Effects of Virtually Addressed Caches on Virtual Memory Design & Performance, *Operating Systems Review*, October 1992, pp 896–908.

[Jouppi 1990] NP Jouppi. Improving Direct-Mapped Cache Performance by the Addition of a Small Fully-Associative Cache and Prefetch Buffers, *Proc. 17th Int. Symp. on Computer Architecture*, Seattle, WA, May 1990, pp 364–373.

[Jouppi 1993] NP Joupi. Cache Write Policies and Performance, *Proc. 20th Int. Symp. on Computer Architecture*, San Diego, CA, May 1993, pp 191–201.

[Kane and Heinrich 1992] G Kane and J Heinrich. *MIPS RISC Architecture*, Prentice-Hall, Englewood Cliffs, NJ, 1992.

[Kernighan and Richie 1978] BW Kernighan and DM Richie. *The C Programming Language*, Prentice-Hall, Englewood Cliffs, NJ, 1978 (2nd edition: 1988).

[Koldinger *et al*. 1991] EJ Koldinger, SJ Eggers and HM Levy. On the Validity of Trace-Driven Simulation for Multiprocessors, *Proc. 18th Int. Symp. on Computer Architecture*, Toronto, May 1991, 244–253.

[Lam *et al*. 1991] MS Lam, EE Rothberg and ME Wolf. The Cache Performance and Optimizations of Blocked Algorithms, *Proc. 4th Int. Conf. on Architectural Support for Programming Languages and Operating Systems*, Santa Clara, CA, 1991, pp 63–74.

[Larus 1993] JR Larus. Efficient Program Tracing, *Computer*, vol. 26 no. 5 May 1993, pp 52–61.

[Lenoski *et al*. 1990] D Lenoski, J Laudon, K Gharachorloo, A Gupta and J Hennessy. The Directory-Based Cache Coherence Protocol for the DASH Multiprocessor, *Proc. 17th Int. Symp. on Computer Architecture*, Seattle, WA, May 1990, pp 148–159.

[Lenoski *et al*. 1992] D Lenoski, J Laudon, K Gharachorloo, W-D Weber, A Gupta, J Hennessy, M Horowitz and MS Lam. The Stanford DASH Multiprocessor, *Computer,* vol. 25 no. 3 March 1992 pp 63–79.

[Lewis 1994] T Lewis. Supercomputers Ain't So Super, *Computer* vol. 27 no. 11 November 1994, pp 5–6.

[Lovett and Thakkar 1988] T Lovett and S Thakkar. The Symmetry Multiprocessor System, *Proc. Int. Conf. of Parallel Processing*, University Park, PA, 1988, pp 303–310.

[Lusk *et al*. 1987] E Lusk, R Overbeek, *et al*. *Portable Programs for Parallel Processors*, Holt, Rinehart and Winston, 1987.

[Machanick 1992] P Machanick. Design of an Object-Oriented Framework for Optimistic Parallel Simulation on Shared-Memory Machines, *South African Computer Journal* no. 6 1992, pp 27–36.

[McDonald 1991] JD McDonald. Particle Simulation in a Multiprocessor Environment, *Proc. AIAA Thermophysics Conf*. Honolulu, Hawaii, June 1991.

[McDonald and Baganoff 1988] JD McDonald and D Baganoff. Vectorization of a Particle Simulation for Hypersonic Rarefied Flow, *Proc. AIAA Thermophysics, Plasmadynamics and Lasers Conf*. June 1988.

[Mellor-Crumney and Scott 1991] JM Mellor-Crumney and ML Scott. Algorithms for Scalable Synchronization on Shared-Memory Multiprocessors, *ACM Trans. on Computer Systems*, vol. 9 no. 1 February 1991, pp 21–65.

[MIPS 1994] *R8000 Microprocessor Chip Set: Product Overview*, MIPS Technologies, Inc., Mountain View, CA, 1994.

[Nagle *et al*. 1993] D Nagle, R Uhlig, T Stanley, S Sechrest, T Mudge and R Brown. Design Trade-Offs for Software Managed TLBs, *Proc. Int. Symp. on Computer Architecture*, May 1993, pp 27–38.

[Prince 1994] B Prince. Memory in the Fast Lane, *IEEE Spectrum*, vol. 31 no. 2 February 1994, pp 38–41.

[Ramanathan and Oren 1993] G Ramanathan and J Oren. Survey of Commercial Parallel Systems, *Computer Architecture News*, vol. 21 No. 3 June 1993, pp 13–33.

[Simmons *et al*. 1992] ML Simmons, HJ Wasserman, OA Lubeck, C Eoyang, R Mendez, H Harada and M Ishiguru. A Performance Comparison of Four Supercomputers, *Communications of the ACM*, vol. 35 no. 8 August 1992, pp 116–124.

[Singh *et al*. 1992a] JP Singh, C Holt, T Totsuka, A Gupta and JL Hennessy. *Load Balancing and Data Locality in Hierarchical N-body Methods*, Technical Report CSL–TR–92–205, Stanford University, February 1992 (latest version: ftp://samay.stanford.edu/papers/nbody-sched.ps.Z).

[Singh *et al*. 1992b] JP Singh, W–D Weber and A Gupta. SPLASH: Stanford Parallel Applications for Shared-Memory, *Computer Architecture News*, vol. 20 no. 1 March 1992, pp 5–44 (latest version: ftp://www-flash.stanford.edu/pub/old_splash/splash/splash.tar.Z).

[Smith 1982] AJ Smith. Cache Memories, *ACM Computing Surveys*, vol. 14 no. 3 September 1982, pp 473–530.

[Snell 1994] M Snell. Supercomputing: Same Name, Different Game, *Computer*, vol. 27 no. 11 November 1994, pp 6–7.

[Snyder 1978] R Snyder. On a Priori Program Restructuring for Virtual Memory Systems, *Proc. 2nd Int. Colloq. on Operating Systems*, October, 1978.

[Sproull and Phillips 1980] RL Sproull and WA Phillips. *Modern Physics* (3rd edition), Wiley, New York 1980.

[Subramanian 1991] I Subramanian. Managing Discardable Pages with an External Pager, *Proc. USENIX Mach* Symposium, November 1991.

[Spirn 1977] JR. Spirn. *Program Behavior: Models and Measurement*, Elsevier/North-Holland, 1977.

[Veenstra 1993] JE Veenstra. *Mint Tutorial and User Manual*, Technical Report 452, Computer Science Department, University of Rochester, June 1993.

[Weber and Gupta 1989] W-D Weber and A Gupta. Analysis of Cache Invalidation Patterns in Multiprocessors, *Proc. 3rd Int. Conf. on Architectural Support for Programming Languages and Operating Systems*, Boston, MA, 1989, pp 243–256.

[Wheeler and Bershad 1992] B Wheeler and B Bershad. Consistency Management for Virtually Indexed Caches, *Proc. 5th Int. Conf. on Architectural Support for Programming Languages and Operating Systems*, Boston, MA, October 1992, pp 124–136.

[Wyatt *et al.* 1992] BB Wyatt, K Kavi and S Hufnagel. Parallelism in Object-Oriented Languages: A Survey, *IEEE Software*, vol. 9 no. 6, November 1992, pp 56–66.

www.ingramcontent.com/pod-product-compliance
Lightning Source LLC
Chambersburg PA
CBHW071152050326
40689CB00011B/2082